# ADVANCE PRAISE FOR
## *STOP SCREAMING AT THE MICROWAVE!*

"Americans are desperately seeking ways to be good workers and good family members at the same time. Mary LoVerde has some first rate solutions, and she understands that "one size does not fit all." This book is about "fanning *your* flame." So what are you waiting for?                    —Linda Ellerbee

*"Stop Screaming at the Microwave!* is a must read for everyone! It will help you balance the complicated and stressful lives we are all leading today."        —Ken Blanchard, coauthor of *The One Minute Manager*

"Erma Bombeck's spirit lives on in Mary LoVerde's funny, insightful book on how to balance your personal and professional life—without losing your mind or your sense of humor. The thought-provoking, life-changing suggestions are illustrated with real-life stories that keep the pages turning and the reader motivated. Men and women, young and old, single and married will all benefit from the author's ideas on how to lead a more congruent life, *now*, not someday."                    —Sam Horn, author of *Tongue Fu!*

"Your ability to focus on the things that really matter will contribute more to your happiness than any other thing you do. This is a wonderful book that gives you a series of practical, proven methods you can use to get more living out of life."
—Brian Tracy, author of *Maximum Achievement: Strategies and Skills That Will Unlock Your Hidden Powers to Succeed*

"An inspirational book, filled with charm, wisdom and wit, reminding us how much we all need each other."
—Paul Pearsall, author of *Heart's Code* and *The Pleasure Prescription*

"I have stopped screaming at the microwave! Thanks to Mary LoVerde for bringing this much needed piece of work into our lives."
—J. Nathan Hill, President, Novus, Greenwood Trust Company

*"Stop Screaming at the Microwave!* has had a profound and lasting effect upon my life. Don't miss this incredible book. It can change your life also!"                    —Mary Jones, President,
Assoc. of Operating Room Nurses Acadiana Chapter

"Mary LoVerde is one of the really special people in life . . . her wit, wisdom and practical ideas are what we all need, and I can't recommend her book highly enough for all of us boomers trying to 'keep it all together'."
—Ron Benirschke, former NFL Man of the Year

# S T O P
# *Screaming*
## at the
# MICROWAVE!

## How to Connect Your

## Disconnected Life

# Mary LoVerde

A FIRESIDE BOOK
*PUBLISHED BY SIMON & SCHUSTER*
New York London Toronto Sydney

FIRESIDE
Rockefeller Center
1230 Avenue of the Americas
New York, NY 10020

For information regarding special discounts for bulk purchases,
please contact Simon & Schuster Special Sales at 1-800-456-6798
or business@simonandschuster.com

Designed by Bonni Leon-Berman

Manufactured in the United States of America

10   9   8   7   6

Library of Congress Cataloging-in-Publication Data
LoVerde, Mary.
   Stop screaming at the microwave! : how to connect your disconnected
life / Mary LoVerde.
      p.   cm.
   1.  Conduct of life.   2.  Quality of life.   I.  Title.
BF637.C5L68   1998
646.7—dc21                    98-22592
ISBN 0-684-85397-3

The author gratefully acknowledges permission from the following sources
to reprint material in their control:
Michael Annison, *Managing the Whirlwind*, Medical Group Management
Association, copyright © 1993.
Joyce Brothers, *The Successful Woman*, Simon & Schuster, copyright © 1988.
Marcia Byalick and Linda Saslow, *The Three Career Couple*, Peterson's,
copyright © 1993. (Available by calling 1-800-338-3282 or through www
.petersons.com)
Anne Morrow Lindbergh, *Gifts from the Sea*, Random House, Inc., copy-
right © 1955.
Price Pritchett, *New Work Habits for a Radically Changing World*, Pritchett
and Associates, copyright © 1994.
Brian Tracy, for quote on page 189.

This book is dedicated to my parents, Tom and Lou Schulte, and my brothers, Tom, Bob, Bill, Greg, and Chuck, who taught me how to connect.

And to Sarah, Emily, and Nicholas, whose love keeps me in balance.

# Acknowledgments

When I began this project I had no idea how many "connections" I'd need. I want to express my love and gratitude to the many people who made this book a reality:

Robert Miller, a true friend in every sense of the word. Thanks for having faith in me and giving me energy.

Jillian Manus, my savvy, brilliant, and kind agent. You said we'd make a great connection and we did.

Becky Cabaza, a writer's dream editor. You read the manuscript and immediately "got it" and then made the polishing process fun.

Sam Horn, an enormously talented author who showed me the ropes and stimulated my creativity. Thanks for caring enough to be compassionately honest.

Lynn Price, founder of Camp To Belong. You are an inspiration beyond words. Thanks for sharing my journey and advising me along the way.

Scott Friedman, my mentor and funniest friend. Thank you for taking me under your wing and teaching and encouraging me.

Mark Sanborn, another mentor and dear friend. You inspire me because of the high standards you set.

Lou Heckler, my incredible speaking coach. Special thanks for the book title, your creative ideas, and for being the best role model I could ever want.

Jonellen Heckler, my favorite author. Thank you for your support and for inspiring me to write.

Juanell Teague, my persistent, innovative business coach. You wouldn't give up "the dig" until I found my profound truth. I am so thankful you believed in me.

Keith and Ann Gay, my wonderful friends who give me a boost whenever I need one in oh so many ways. Thanks for lifting me up.

Barbara Lubbers, my trainer and loving friend. Thanks for listening and helping me develop ideas, even when it meant taking a pad of paper on our workouts.

Eric Chester, Melanie Mills, and Brian O'Malley, part of the Magnificent Seven. You challenged and stretched me and so generously gave me great ideas.

Debbie Taylor, my world-class assistant, who lived part-time at the post office and in cyberspace while I wrote. There would be no book without you.

Bev Kelly, my other dedicated assistant. You are like part of the family.

Wes Hempel, my fabulous artist friend. Special thanks for so generously letting your paint dry and your deadlines wait while you taught me to write.

Stan Rabbe, Jim Estey, Mary Jones, Neal McChristy, Connie Asher, Kay Allenbaugh, Judy Anderson, Greg Rudy, Jeff Baenen, Kay Czarnecki, Roswitha Smale, Mike Bewley, Mark Mitcheltree, and Mary and Rolf Bernirschke. Thanks for your support and for coming into my life at just the moment I needed you.

My audience members, especially my Chapman University students in Hawaii and the members of the Association of Operating Room Nurses. I am forever grateful for the lessons you teach me.

My friends and colleagues, who read the manuscript and gave me invaluable feedback.

Brenda Abdilla, my cherished friend. I am sure you were sent by my guardian angel.

And most of all, to Sarah, Emily, and Nicholas. I love you with all my heart.

# Contents

PART IV
# Connecting with the Big Picture

# Getting
# Started

# CHAPTER 1

# When You Can't Keep Up

Hurried and worried until we are buried,
and there's no curtain call,
Life is a very funny proposition, after all.
—*George M. Cohan*

I got home from work and flopped into my easy chair, totally exhausted. I turned on the answering machine and heard the baby-sitter for my (then) five-year-old son Nicholas. She explained how she had driven him to preschool that morning, walked into the classroom and saw before her nineteen little boys and girls, all sitting in a circle, wiggling with excitement, and . . . she noticed, each one of them was wearing a Halloween costume.

All of them except Nicholas.

She went on to describe (in brutal detail) how he had burst into tears, clung to her leg, and begged to go home.

OK. So Mother of the Year I wasn't. In fact, I felt like the worst parent on the planet. Despite my best efforts to keep all those plates spinning, I had let one fall. I had humiliated my child in front of his friends. I felt overwhelmed and exhausted, and I vowed then and there I would never let my life get so out of balance again.

But how? I had tried the superperson route and had failed. Yes, there were some days I could pull it off, sometimes even for days in a row. *I just couldn't keep it up.* I needed something a little more realistic. Surely there was a better way. (There is.)

## We're All in the Same Boat

You might see yourself in this story. Whether it is failing to meet the needs of your family or failing to get it all done at work, many of us feel like we are doing just that: *failing.* No matter how hard we plan or work, it never seems to be enough.

We aren't alone. According to the National Study on the Changing Workforce, Americans are overwhelmed, exhausted, and constantly under stress from trying to accomplish more than we can handle. If you feel that you have too much to do and not enough time to do it, well, you are not imagining it. Actually, you are not in this predicament because you are failing in some way. There really is too much to do. We know we can't keep up. We are going 90 miles an hour and the faster we go, the farther behind we get.

Do you remember the *Leave It to Beaver* show? To many of us baby boomers who grew up with the show, the Cleavers were the perfect family. Part of our current frustration stems from the fact that we still cling to the "Cleaver ideal." Don't get me wrong: I have a lot of June Cleaver in me. I believe in the values we associate with that model. However, I discovered I was trying to run my life according to Cleaver Principles. I believed things like:

- I can solve all problems in thirty minutes.
- The division of labor between men and women is equal and agreed upon.
- I can always "be there."
- My idea of a juvenile delinquent was Eddie Haskell!

We live in a very different world than June and Ward experienced. In America, women now make up more than 50 percent of the workforce. One in two marriages ends in divorce. We have biological, open adoptive, single, joint-custody, step, foster, and surrogate mothers. We have in vitro, latchkey, and boomerang kids. And a dozen flavors of deadbeat, Disneyland, and dedicated dads. The Cleavers we're not. That doesn't mean family life has gone to hell in a handbasket. It means that we can believe in the values of days gone by—with the understanding that our lives probably won't look like June and Ward's.

## We Disconnect in the Name of Balance

I once listened to a man proudly announce that he was "going at *breakneck* speed to meet his *dead*line." I had a gut-wretching response to his words. I prayed his body would not obey his vicious command. I started listening carefully to how we describe our lives. I was flabbergasted at the language! Ask someone, "How are you?" and she might respond:

- "I'm *hanging* in there." Is she saying she needs a *lifeline*, not a noose?
- "I'm *torn* in a million directions." Would she rather be *centered* in one direction?
- "I am coming *apart* at the seams." Does she want her connections *intact*?
- "I am *pulled* in a dozen ways." Could she really be pleading to have her life together in one "peace"?

I was astonished to hear how we felt *hung, torn,* and *pulled apart.* Such pain! It sounded like I was on the set of the popular nineties television drama *ER*!

I could hear the cry for unity. We hurt and we attempt to relieve our psychic pain by disconnecting.

## We Disconnect from Ourselves

First, we separate from our bodies. This is like ignoring the advice of a loyal devoted friend. Our bodies tell us when things are out of kilter. Initially, it informs us nicely; we get tired, thirsty, hungry, achy, short of breath, forgetful, or irritable—and our pants get tight. Then, if we take no action, it talks louder and more urgently; we get ulcers, insomnia, headaches, chest pains, rashes, panic attacks—and our pants get tighter. As a last resort, our bodies make final attempts to get our attention; we get heart disease, diabetes, hypertension, cancer, emphysema—and our pants no longer fit at all. As the former director of the Hypertension Research Center at the University of Colorado, I saw patients regularly who insisted they had no symptoms before their heart attack, stroke, or bout with gout. In fact, we called hypertension the "silent killer" because people did not know anything was wrong.

How ridiculous! Of course our bodies talk to us—over and over again. We have taught ourselves to override the early detection system that protects us. We rob ourselves of a healthy diet, adequate exercise, enough sleep, and good medical care because "we don't have time." We ignore our bodies in the name of balance and end up with a butt-related depression. Even our Wonder Bras have a limit to the miracles they can perform. We can't fool Mother Nature.

## We Disconnect from Our Families

I will never forget the day I was at the computer, feeling pestered by the kids, when I shouted, "Leave me alone! Can't you see I am writing a book about connection?" Immediately thereafter, I developed a case of guilty writer's block. Who could blame me? Once again, in my zeal to get it all done, I disengaged from who I was and how I wanted to be. And I am not the only one who acts this way. My audience members tell me how they stay up late completing all the chores and end up too tired to hear about the delights of the day. They confess that their conversations deteriorate into "Who's picking up the kids?" "Can you get the shirts from the laundry?" "Your mother called—again." They describe how they work hard to buy things that will make them look sexy and attractive, and then are too tired for romance. We disengage from what feels good. (And we still don't get it all done.)

## We Disconnect from Others

Many of us could sit down right now and make a list of fifteen friends who we genuinely enjoy but haven't contacted in months, maybe even years. When we get overwhelmed we often cut out the very people who could help us the most: the ones who encourage, stimulate, and challenge us; the ones who know us warts and all and like us anyway; and especially those fun, zany friends who always make us laugh. God knows we could all use a good laugh. But we decide we are too busy right now and so we put our noses to the grindstone and try to solve our problems in a vacuum.

## We Disconnect with the Big Picture

Feeling this disjointed, we can't find our way in the world. We doubt ourselves and our God. It is unsettling to be so out of touch. We want sublime balance and end up with confusion and uneasiness. Some of us lose hope.

## What They Said Would Work . . . Doesn't

Ironically, many of the strategies we use to find balance actually disconnect us—making us feel even worse. In an attempt to get everything completed we lock out our true emotions and shut ourselves off from who we really are and what we really want. The isolation and frenetic pace we create can literally make us sick. The sad part is that our valiant efforts don't work anyway—there is still too much to do.

### We Tried Time Management

Many time-management ideas are invaluable and I use them regularly. The problem with this strategy, however, is that for every hour that I allegedly "save," I have ten hours of demands competing for it. Many of us focus on our bottomless to-do lists, frustrated that there is never enough time—and we are right—we will never get more than twenty-four hours a day. So we speed up.

I read on the sports page this summer about a race car driver who, in a risky strategic maneuver, skipped the scheduled pit stop to try to win the race. His plan worked and he narrowly won—and then he ran out of gas in the victory lap and had to be pushed back in. Isn't that exactly what some of us do? We maximize every minute, refusing to pull over for a pit stop so we can win our "race," and then we run out of gas on our victory lap: too exhausted to have fun on the weekends, too distracted to enjoy our evenings, or too full of health problems to savor our retirement.

"Time" itself is now controversial and the experts can't seem to agree on the truth about time. Some time-management researchers say we have more leisure time than ever. Others declare we could go home if we wanted to but work is so appealing and home so chaotic, we actually prefer the office. All this flies in the face of what real people tell me: "I don't have time for the important things in my life."

Whatever the real truth about time is, the perception by most is that we are out of sync. I believe the conflicting reports stem from the fact that time is not really the source of our dissatisfaction. We are disconnecting to cope—and that is the opposite of what it will take to achieve harmony.

## Is Living in the Moment the Answer?

I don't think so. I wish I were better at this. I know I could get a lot out of cherishing each minute but frankly, at some moments I want to: a) burst into tears and crawl into bed; b) eat the whole container of Häagen-Dazs; or c) ram the car ahead of me (not real hard, just enough to get the guy to go a *little* faster). If I focused on those moments I would definitely be disconnected . . . or so the officer explained.

## What About Prioritizing?

Many experts tell us to live according to our priorities. OK, I'm game. So how do I do that? I understand and admire the concept of "first things first," but how do I use this advice on a day-to-day basis? I have a difficult time even ranking my priorities, and I bet you do, too. Is going to work my top choice so we don't lose the house? Is it more important to stay home with my child with the croup? (Only soon we wouldn't have any place in which to "stay home.") Or maybe I should call in sick and go to the gym and exercise because if I have a heart attack and die I can't pay the mortgage or raise a child. I

know I have to live my life according to what's important—
and I try. It's just that I'm not sure on an hourly basis exactly
what that looks like. On my hassled harried days I want to
scream, "Which things first?" I can get bogged down trying
to make every decision based on priorities. And it doesn't feel
good. I second-guess myself and feel guilty for choosing one
priority over the other.

### Keep It Simple, Stupid

I also tried to simplify. I especially enjoyed Sarah Ban
Breathnach's lovely book, *Simple Abundance*. Her strategies did
help. But no matter how simple I made my life, complicated
problems kept cropping up. The solutions to the problems
weren't so easy to implement, either. The other barrier: I was
not a great student of the craft. I did not want to ride the bus
to my children's orthodontist, stop dry-cleaning my wool suits,
or collect rainwater to wash my hair. I was the remedial reader
of the simplicity movement. I discovered I could streamline
my life but sometimes that took away the things I really liked.
And there was a limit to how much I could cut out of my
modern urban life. Taken to an extreme, I felt unattractive,
dull, and muddled. My life was simple—and boring.

### Is the Secret to Just Get Organized and Delegate?

My problem is not *getting* organized—it is *staying* organized.
I don't know exactly where those piles come from, but no
sooner do I get one down than another mysteriously pops up.
I could devote my life to pile reduction. I tried that but just
didn't find much levity in it. I finally got all my ducks in a row
and then I realized I don't like ducks!

I also learned that my dependence on organization made
me think I could have more and more things—"I'll find a

place for it." It reminded me of the Zen masters who teach that when we set our material standards so high, we are held in bondage by the things we ourselves hold in bondage. I hate to think of the weekends I've wasted sorting "stuff" that held me captive in my closet.

I am also the master of delegating. I can take what is on my desk and dump it on someone else's in the time it takes to say, "You do it." The gambit often works—for a while. Then I get back to my office and find that the voice mail is full of requests and the heaps start again. Giving it to someone else didn't make me feel better. It didn't get me home any earlier or earn me more money or make me any friends. It did not connect me with anyone or anything.

I also wrote mission statements, made pie charts, and read my daily horoscope. I juggled until I was black and blue, and still I lagged behind. While all the strategies helped, they were not enough. I still hurt.

## Time for a New Solution

Most of the strategies for balancing your work and home life focus on how to do more: work harder and faster and sleep less. We don't need to know how to do *more*. As one woman wrote to me, "I feel like a stretched rubber band about ready to pop." And we don't need government statistics, research findings, or fifty-two exciting ways to make chicken (after all, Domino's delivers).

We are smart. We know that our demands at work are not going to lessen, little elves are not going to suddenly start cleaning the bathroom, and an hour of daily, uninterrupted leisure time is not going to be a reality anytime soon. What we want most now is to experience some joy. We are tired of being tired. Many of us haven't felt good in a long time. This lack of excitement in our lives is a particularly bitter pill to swallow for a generation who grew up with the motto "If it feels good, do it."

We are desperately searching for ways to feel good. We buy Prozac in the convenient fifty-five-gallon-drum size, we channel-surf looking for something to entertain us, and we use retail therapy to buy some happiness. It is not hard to understand the recent increase in heroin overdoses, our debt-ridden society, or the epidemic of depression. In my fifteen years as a faculty member at the University of Colorado Medical School, I often summarized my job description as "find the pain and fix it." I believe we have to do the same thing to cure ourselves. Instead of just medicating ourselves, we have the power to restore our natural joy.

It is not easy to shed our old ways. But we must. Michael Annison, author of *Managing the Whirlwind*, said, "Because many of the rules of the past no longer apply, doing what we have always done is a prescription for disaster." He concluded,

"If you are going in the wrong direction, speeding up doesn't help."

Although he was offering business advice, his wisdom applies to our personal lives as well. I believe concentrating on to-do lists and doing more—faster and faster and harder and harder—is definitely a step in the wrong direction. I've concluded:

Our problem is not a need for speed, it's a correction of direction.

## OK. So What's Your Point?

We've learned the hard way that what we have tried hasn't worked. We have done everything we could including jumping through burning hoops and we have made little or no progress. I believe that unless we learn to connect, no amount of managing, organizing, delegating, prioritizing, or simplifying will make us feel good.

Feeling good is what balance is all about.

## The Best Blueprint for Balance: Connection

Disconnection causes our pain. Connection will relieve it. Our game plan for living the good life must focus on *connecting* because it will exhilarate us in ways that clean houses, completed projects, or even cold, hard cash never can. It is time to come to a new realization:

Connection creates balance.

It may be the bonds you make with your spouse and family or your friends and colleagues. It may be relating to those countless strangers you meet every day. It may be the inner peace you make with yourself when you meditate, pray, or allow yourself to enjoy nature or experience silence. Or it may be the communion you feel when you connect spiritually. In moments of sheer exhaustion and maddening stress, it is these bonds that will make us whole again.

It is time to start viewing life balance in a different light. The new life balance motto is:

When you can't keep up, connect.

## What Is Connection? How Do I Use It to Balance My Life?

Defining connection is like trying to explain love, peace, or justice. Such complex and intense feelings are hard to articulate. I asked my good friend "Webster" for help and found many definitions. Let's take a look at them and see how they relate to balance.

---

CONNECTION IS DEFINED AS:

*The relation between things that depend on, involve, or follow each other; a causal relationship.*

---

Barbara Lubbers, a personal trainer and fitness guru, told me about a valuable lesson she learned. She said, "I understood what you meant about connecting when I visited my husband, Steve, at his office one day. He was speaking with a customer and neither of them saw me walk up. I heard the man ask my husband, 'How's Barbara?' Steve answered, 'For someone who doesn't work full-time she is the busiest damn person I have ever met.' They noticed me just then and we all had a good laugh, but later his words hit me like a brick. I was shocked at his message. Despite my weekly volunteer work at the hospice, my herculean efforts to be a good mom, and my dedication at the gym and my church, I was disconnected from my husband. He was saying I didn't have enough time for the most important relationship in my life."

Barbara and Steve realized that they need to depend on each other and to be intertwined in each other's lives. Despite successful businesses and a desire to serve others, they couldn't find true balance without relating to one another. Living in the same house or even working side by side doesn't guarantee togetherness. Connection requires *involvement*.

> CONNECTION IS ALSO DEFINED AS:
>
> *The act or means of transferring from one train or bus, etc., to another in the course of a journey.*

Scott Friedman, my mentor and the funniest humorist I know, showed me how this definition can help us in our daily decision-making. Scott invited me to cohost a party with him for twenty of our mutual business associates. The only date available was Yom Kippur, the holiest day of the Jewish calendar. He casually said, "But that's OK. I'll simply tell my family I've made other plans. They will just have to understand this is the only night we can have our dinner."

About two weeks before the party, with all the plans made and invitations sent, Scott called to say he would not be able to cohost after all.

"Scott!" I lamented, "You can't bail out on me now!"

"I am really sorry, but actually it's all your fault."

Scott is a pretty funny guy so I couldn't wait to hear how I could be to blame. "It's those questions you taught me to ask. When I asked, 'What should I do?' the answer was, 'Keep my commitment to you.' But when I asked, 'With whom do I need to connect?' the answer came loud and clear. My Jewish faith grounds me. As a bachelor I need to be reminded who I am, where I come from, and who I can count on. I love living a single man's jet-setting lifestyle, but without my Jewish traditions, beliefs, and family experiences I would be lost. I need to be with my family for dinner that night. I have to say I am surprised at my decision. At first I didn't think it would be any big deal to miss the holiday celebration, but it just didn't feel right. Now I understand why."

Scott is absolutely correct. Our connections help us find our way in this trip we call life. They take us where we want to go. David Nichols wrote, "Without connection, there is something dangerous and wrong about the world." I agree. I also believe the converse is true. If we emphasize our connections, we stay on track, the world seems less scary, and we can find our true sources of joy and comfort. Many of us may be like Scott, surprised at the places we find those connections.

### There's More
I then read the meaning of "connect."

---

**TO CONNECT MEANS:**
*To plug into an electrical current.*

---

I was in a San Francisco hotel, resting up after a long day of speaking engagements and client meetings, when I got the call from my husband. He very excitedly related the events of the day. While our daughter Emily was at a movie, a young man in her class named Adam placed a ten-foot homemade sign on our garage door that said, "Homecoming '97—Adam?" Then he lined the driveway and the sidewalk all the way up to the front door with chocolate kisses. On the doorstep he placed a red rose and a note that said, "Now that I have 'kissed' the ground you walk on, will you go to the homecoming dance with me?"

Emily got on the phone squealing with excitement and filled me in on the details.

My first response was, "Emily, I just have one thing to say: Marry him."

Now I realize she is only fourteen years old, but correct me if I am wrong—she could do worse.

When I hung up the phone my heart sank. I missed it! I

should have been there! What kind of parent am I? There was that Cleaver principle rearing its guilty head again. I stopped myself and asked, "But where is the *problem*?"

Everyone was turned on! It was as though we were all plugged into an electric current. Emily was tingling and floating on air. Adam was ecstatic—the girl had said yes! His mother (who had driven him over and was sitting in the car while her son made his rite of passage) was grinning from ear to ear. It wasn't so long ago she couldn't get him to take a shower and now he was Romeo asking Juliet for a date. My husband was having a ball being totally obnoxious with the video camera. *Everyone was connected.* To be honest, I was having a few magical moments of my own in San Francisco, hooking up with an old friend for dinner and feeling very in tune with my audience, doing what I love to do.

When I viewed the situation from a "connection" point of view, I couldn't find a problem. There was nothing to feel bad about.

The next week Emily and I are out shopping for the perfect dress, matching shoes, and a slip that doesn't show. I am talking about how happy I am that she was asked to the homecoming dance in such a clever and romantic way when she stops in the middle of the mall, puts her hands on her hips, looks at me warily, and says, "You're going to use this story in your talks, aren't you?"

I already had. We were so close she knew me. She understood I couldn't pass up a tale this good. My heart warmed because she had me pegged. Doesn't that turn us on—when someone we love knows us so well that he or she can predict what we will probably say or do? I realized I hadn't missed anything. The experience was a turn-on for all of us. The connection was electrifying.

(For those of you who, like Paul Harvey, want the rest of the story, I can tell you they had a wonderful time at the dance and Emily looked like a supermodel. Unfortunately she decided not to marry Adam. I've secretly kept his number so if she ever changes her mind . . .)

I believe the next definition explains why connection so powerfully balances our lives.

---

TO CONNECT MEANS:

*To reach the thing aimed at.* (Like hitting a ball or a target solidly.)

---

We accomplish our goals and attain our dreams when we connect. Isn't that, after all, what we are really trying to do? We connect when we "reach" what or whom we are aiming at: ourselves, our family, our world, and our spirituality.

Melanie Mills, president of Higher Ground Training and Development, Inc., told me, "Connection is that moment when I am aware of being present and fully available to the situation at hand. It is the spontaneous moment that reminds me I am alive and well and there is much for which I am grateful. It is the gentle times when I choose to let someone ease into my traffic lane, notice the colors of the sunset, or hold my honey before drifting off to sleep. It is when I hear my own breath while exercising, make eye contact with a stranger and exchange a gentle smile, send a card for no reason, sing on a friend's voice mail, or cry while watching *Oprah*. I feel connected when I am real, authentic, and fully engaged. How do I stay connected? By following my hunches and acting on my instincts in the very moment they speak to me."

I couldn't have said it better myself.

## I Like All This Emotional Feel-Good Stuff, but How Do I Get It All Done?

When I ask my clients how they cope with multiple demands, they throw up their hands and shrug. Tom Christal, president of a food brokerage company in San Antonio, told me matter-of-factly, "I could work twenty-four hours a day, seven days a week and still not get it all finished." He's right. Most of us couldn't get everything accomplished with a fairy's wand.

So how *do* you get it all done?

You don't. It is no longer a realistic expectation. Each morning I prepare my to-do list and it often looks something like this:

1. Make dentist appointment for Emily
2. Finish notes for Friday's keynote
3. Rewrite presentation for new client
4. Shop for Saturday's birthday party
5. Prepare monthly accounting
6. Return calls and e-mail
7. Get milk
8. Arrange travel for next month's trips

. . . and so on and so on . . . up to twenty tasks. I prioritize the twenty things itemized on my pad—A,B,C—and all of them are an A. We have been out of milk for four days. My accountant has called three times for my accounting information to meet the filing deadline. Emily has a toothache. The airfare goes up unless I book the trips today. I can feel my blood pressure rising. I know I can't get all twenty things accomplished today so I start to stress out.

The fact is, I can probably get eight of them done. I can "do

them disconnected" (and feel bad) or I can "do them connected" (and feel good). Either way, eight is it. For you, the
number might be twenty or ten or five. But by now I hope
you're beginning to realize the importance of doing things in
a connected way. You can cut your list down to size *and* get
connected by doing the following:

## Ask the Four Questions

Before I leave on a business trip I have forty-seven things to
do. As I prepare, I ask myself four questions. For example:

Q. What *should* I do before I leave?
A. Go to the charity board of director's meeting.

Q. What do I *want* to do?
A. Exercise.

Q. What do I *need* to do?
A. Wash the clothes so the family will have some clean underwear while I'm gone.

Then I ask the most important question:

### With whom should I *connect*?

I realize that I will be gone for several nights. I remember that
my daughter and I had a spat last evening and what will make
me feel better is doing something fun together before I leave.
So the answer is easy: my daughter Emily. The charity's board
of directors will forgive me (or get over it), I can exercise on
the road, and clean underwear every day is an overrated concept. (I mean, who is going to ever know?)

The next week on the road I will ask the same four questions:

Q. What *should* I do?

A. Return the twenty-two calls that have come in since I was gone.

Q. What do I *want* to do?

A. Sleep.

Q. What do I *need* to do?

A. Call home.

Q. With whom should I *connect*?

A. My audience. This is their "opening night" and I must give them my undivided attention.

And the following week the answer to the last question will be: myself. I'll exercise and get some extra sleep. My body has served me well and I owe it much gratitude. Fully rested, I will launch an attack on that ever-growing paper pile.

The next time you are faced with too much to do and not enough time to do it, try asking the four questions:

---

### THE CONNECTION SOLUTION

1. What *should* I do?
2. What do I *want* to do?
3. What do I *need* to do?
4. With whom should I *connect?*

---

## My Connection with You

Here are the facts. We will not ever, ever, *ever* again get everything completed. We will never say, "I think I will go to bed now because I can't think of a single thing I need to do." No one will thank us for our efforts at work and insist, "Why don't you take the rest of the week off? You've made our company enough money for this month." We won't live like Ward and June did, have lifelong job security, or revert back to the good old days. Nevertheless, we can live a passionate, peaceful, purposeful, and—yes—balanced life if we learn to relate, bond, and get turned on. This book is designed to help you do precisely that.

I arranged this book to make it very easy for you to use the ideas. You will find four parts: Connecting with Yourself, Connecting with Your Family, Connecting with Others, and Connecting with the Big Picture. The order is deliberate. I believe we must begin with ourselves and then link up with the people we are closest to before we can continue outward. I wrote the chapters so the light shines directly on you. Throughout this process, I want you to ask yourself, "What makes me disconnected?" "What can I do to feel more connected?" "What can I change?"

I also want to make it easy for you to get started. Beginning in Part I of this book, each chapter ends with suggestions to help you get past your barriers. You'll find:

1. **The New Solution,** encouraging you to reevaluate how you are handling common problems and to zero in on using connection.
2. **Microactions,** containing a list of steps you might take. (The concept of microactions will be explained in chapter 3.)
3. **In Real Life,** featuring an inspiring letter from someone who has successfully used the strategies described in the chapter.

My fervent wish is that you will find many ideas you'll want to implement immediately.

## I Think I Can. I Think I Can. I Think I Can.

I know the concepts in this book can work for you. Applying these simple principles, tens of thousands of people have improved their lives. You can, too! It's easier than you might think. Dare to make changes. Dare to become your best self.

### The Halloween Story, Continued . . .

So I am sitting there with tears streaming down my face, as I listen to the heinous crime I have committed by failing to send my child to school properly costumed. On the food chain, I feel like I am one step above the common garden slug. I am sure any minute Social Services is going to ring the doorbell and revoke my parenting permit.

The doorbell does ring, but instead of Social Services, it is Nicholas home from preschool. I took one look at his sweet face, and said, "Oh, honey, I am so very sorry for forgetting your costume."

"Oh yeah, Mom, it was awful! I cried and I cried. But then I found out: YOU GET CANDY ANYWAY!"

"You know what you have, Nick? You have a mom who feels really bad for forgetting your costume. But you know what I have? I have the neatest little boy in the world."

He shrugged, then threw his arms around me. "Oh, Mom," he told me. "Don't worry about it. I still love you."

I knew then what balance was all about.

We don't need a costume.

We don't have to be perfect.

And we do not have to get "it" all done.

All we have to do is. . . . *connect.*

# CHAPTER 2

# Connection Is for Everyone

*In every person, even in such as appear most reckless, there is an inherent desire to attain balance.*
—*Jakob Wassermann*

If you are like my audiences, you may have a few "Yes, but . . ." questions you'd like answered. Let's cover those now.

## Yes, But . . .
## Isn't This Just a Woman's Issue?

Despite what I consider to be overwhelming evidence to the contrary, I am still often rebuked, "Let's get real. Men aren't going to get into this 'connection creates balance' approach, are they?"

I had the privilege of speaking to four hundred actuaries at their annual convention. It was a primarily male audience and

I was forewarned by many. "What a tough audience! Don't worry if your ideas don't go over because they are a very analytical, business-oriented audience and may not embrace your philosophy." I delivered the keynote address without changing a word. My remarks seemed well received, but I knew the true test would be the breakout session immediately following.

To my surprise and delight the room was packed—with men! I asked them to share their connection strategies with the group. Bill, a seemingly quiet, reserved man in his forties, spoke up first, and his idea was so compelling that when he finished, the audience broke into spontaneous applause. The session was incredible. After his brave precedent, the other men felt safe to "confess" their ideas, too. Later, Bill wrote to me and explained his story in detail:

> Dear Mary,
>
> A couple of years ago I went through a very painful divorce. When faced with the prospect of spending the Christmas holiday alone for the first time in my life, I came upon a method of having the people I cared for be with me on Christmas.
>
> For months before Christmas I made a point of calling my extended family members and friends, and asking them to each send a Christmas ornament which I could hang on my tree. The ornament would always remind me of them.
>
> As each ornament arrived, I recorded it in a little journal which I keep in the ornament box. Each of them seemed special, and it gave me a warm feeling as each person responded. While I had been worrying about "bothering" people with this request, I found that, in-

stead, they all seemed to actually enjoy the process of choosing a meaningful ornament. In fact, many of them sent more in the second year, without being asked. Some family members (like my mother and brother) made a special trip together to choose their ornaments.

One ornament stood out in particular. I will quote my Christmas letter for the following year:

Last year, I asked most of my friends and relatives to help me feel more connected at Christmas by giving me an ornament I could put on my tree. The response was really wonderful. I've kept track of them in a book which I will keep from year to year. I took a picture of it, and that is the Christmas card enclosed with this letter.

At the top of the tree you can see a special ornament. Among those who agreed to give me an ornament was my uncle Bob. I heard for weeks that he was making an ornament in his shop. When I opened the package with his ornament, it impacted me so much that I had tears rolling down my cheeks. There are two reasons: 1) My uncle Bob was a very special person in my life. He was almost the only adult male in my childhood that was nurturing, accepting and loving. He always will have a big place in my heart. 2) The ornament was a handmade reproduction of the front of my grandparents' cottage in Stockbridge, a place that holds magical memories for my brother, sister, and me.

I hope you find this useful.
Sincerely,
Bill Bluhm
Actuary, Milliman and Robertson, Inc.

### Cow Dung

I also spoke at the American Farm Bureau national convention. My breakout session was opposite "Manure Management: Does It Cost or Pay?" Farmers, 1,800 in all, showed up for my program. I decided that if the farmers would forgo fertilizer information and the actuaries would write letters about Christmas ornaments, we can put to rest our doubts about men wanting a better life. For those who disagree, I think they are seriously underestimating men.

## Yes, But . . . What About the Bottom Line?

I often hear from interested businesspeople who chide, "This is all good and well for us personally, but it is a jungle out there in the business world. Our company is facing ruthless competition and profits mean everything. Will staying balanced through connection impact our business well-being?"

Good question. And I believe the answer is: You bet your bottom line it will. A *USA Today* survey found that balancing work and home life was a major concern for 75 percent of CEOs and 88 percent of middle managers. That is a hard statistic to ignore. Business experts tell us that a major concern of 88 percent of management will affect profits.

### Karoshi

We have seen what work-life struggles did to the Japanese economy. We have been following the Japanese management and productivity models for years now, hoping to emulate their success. We all know their economy has suffered a downturn. The reasons are many, but when the economists studied the problem they were surprised that a major factor in their downturn was a concept called *karoshi*. It means "death from overwork." The economists noted that the men left for work early in the morning, returned late at night, and had essentially little contact with their families. They concluded that "a booming economy fraught with social tension is destined to be short-lived."

## A Tried and True Taxi

I experience the power of connection in business every time my regular cabdriver, Doug Wiermaa, drives me home from the airport. He specializes in prompt, friendly service in an immaculate car. In addition to that, he knows the "drill": where to pick me up, where to put my luggage, what music I like to listen to, how to get to my house, etc. He can sense whether to let me rant about the perils of travel or sit in exhausted silence. When he drives me home his service forms a buffer between the chaotic life of planes, trains, and automobiles and the reentry into my personal life. He creates an environment that connects me with myself before I walk in the front door. He is an incredibly important link in my life and worth every penny he charges. I asked him one day, "By the way, what's the name of your company?"

He said, "Express Connections."

I wasn't surprised.

## It Makes Sense

Today's fierce business climate intensifies our need to work at peak levels. Stratford Sherman wrote in *Fortune* magazine, "Global competition demands the best of us. Getting centered has never been more important." I asked Robert Schwarze, president and CEO of the Association of Sales and Marketing Companies, how he thought the concept of "balance through connection" applied to business. He said, "In these rapidly changing times I need to connect with my family more than ever before. I need them to help me relax, to feel loved, and to know that someone really cares about me. The connection with them is important to justify why I am working so hard and doing all these crazy things. After all, I want my efforts to benefit my family. In addition, I know it works the other way, too. Their love energizes me. Being connected to them makes me a better CEO. Seeing this big picture gives me a greater appreciation of the pressures my own people are under."

I couldn't agree more. And so for many of us, working in industries with unprecedented degrees of rapid change, stiff competition, and narrowing profit margins on a global basis, balancing our work, family, and personal life through connection makes very good business sense.

## Yes, But . . . I'm Not Married and I Don't Have Kids. Will This Still Work?

In each chapter you will read many different strategies for staying connected. Don't think of this book as everything you'll ever need to know about connection. Instead, think of it as an all-you-can-eat buffet. Go through the line and serve yourself the ideas that look the best to you, and sample some you might not have tried before. Many of the stories are about my experiences, stories that revolve around being a happily married mother of three who makes a living as a speaker and writer. But I don't want you to hear only *my* story. I want you to hear *your* story. The principles of connection apply to everyone—men, women, married, single, divorced, young, or old. It doesn't matter if you are more like Murphy Brown, Michael Jordan, or Old Mother Hubbard. Take the ideas and turn them upside down, right side up, sideways, and every which way to make them work in your life.

# PART I
# *Connecting*
## with
# Yourself

# CHAPTER 3

# Microactions: Inch by Inch

Check the distance between your lips and your life.
—*Mark Sanborn*

Look at your life. Are you living it according to your values? The first step in tuning up your life is to look at your circumstances and ask, "What is the distance between what I say I believe in and what I actually do?" The answer will give you a handle on what needs to change. We begin here because putting life in order requires change.

We all want to live our lives according to our values—to do what is really important. So if we profess to put our family first, if we desperately want some time for ourselves, and we know we should exercise—why don't we do it?

Beats me.

The best minds in history have wrestled with the issue of human behavior modification. No one has found a foolproof way to get humans to change. We seem to have an invisible barrier that often prevents us from doing what we know is good for us.

I have found an interesting way around it. Called microactions, these teeny, tiny steps propel us forward without threatening our sense of control. We all hate to be told what to do —even if we are telling ourselves. We need to outfox our resistance to change.

Microactions have become the cornerstone of my own attempts at balance. "Steps" did not always work for me. They seemed too big because they required that I give up control, make a commitment, and risk failure. (These are not my three favorite things to do.) Microactions get around my fears because I stay in control, commit to something so small I could hardly fear it, and I am guaranteed success.

I am surprisingly easy to outsmart.

## The Two Hardest Things to Do: Lose Weight and Save Money

I first learned about the power of microactions when I used the concept to help my patients make dramatic changes. As the director of the Hypertension Research Center at the University of Colorado, I tested a new drug to treat obesity. The research volunteers were significantly overweight and, by definition, nonexercisers. To participate in the study, the patient agreed to adopt a low-fat diet, take the study pill daily, and exercise at least three times a week. As you can imagine, the "exercise three times a week" was the least compliant portion of the study.

One patient in particular really struggled. She hated to exercise. I honestly think she'd rather wire her jaw shut, staple her stomach, or eat a strict diet of earthworms. At each weekly visit I'd write her exercise prescription (walk for thirty minutes three times a week after work). At each return visit she'd confess she had not exercised at all. We tried every behavior modification trick in the book—rewards, punishments, meditations, affirmations. You name it, we tried it. Nothing worked. Then we tried a microaction.

## Calorie Burners

I asked her if she could simply *get dressed to exercise* three times a week. I gave her explicit instructions NOT to exercise, just get dressed. She laughed in my face. "What a worthless thing to do! Let me get this straight. I'm suppose to come home from work and just get dressed to exercise? A sweatshirt will not burn any calories!"

"I agree. But this week, I am asking you to humor me."

One week later she returned. I asked her if she had complied with the "just get dressed" prescription.

"Yes, I did."

"Great! Next week I'd like you to add one minute of walk-ing—"

She interrupted me with a sheepish grin. "I walked for twenty minutes three times this week."

"But I gave you strict instructions that you did not have to. And you said you hate to exercise. What happened?"

She laughed. "I felt so stupid standing there, all dressed up with no place to go, that I decided to walk just a little. Before I knew it I was five blocks from home. I found out walking isn't so bad. The next time my neighbor saw me and asked if she could join me. Now I have a walking buddy. We chat the whole way, and between the hiking and the verbal venting, I feel like a new person when I get back. You won't believe this, but I look forward to those trips now."

Microactions really work. I use them on myself all the time. For example, I want to do two hundred sit-ups a day: one hundred first thing in the morning and one hundred the last thing at night. (I do them unassisted. I'm the only person in America without an "Ab Roller.") My goal is 1,400 a week. Can I commit to 1,400 sit-ups a week? Not on your life. So I tell myself I have to do only one sit-up.

Who can't do one sit-up? I do one and then while I'm down

there I do ninety-nine more. I don't dislike doing sit-ups, I dislike *thinking* about making myself do sit-ups. I hate the feeling I *must* do them and that if I don't, I am somehow "bad." So I trick myself into it and get past the barrier.

Do I do 1,400 every week? Of course not. Some days I do one sit-up twice a day. Sometimes I do twenty-five. And, I am proud to say, sometimes I do two hundred.

## Ben Franklin Was Wrong

A penny saved is not a penny earned. At 10 percent interest, it is 2.6 cents in just ten years. In twenty it is 6.7 cents and in thirty years it is 17.4 cents.

You know about compound interest. Yet, do you save enough money each year? Me neither. Saving money is a perfect example of microactions. Curt Anderson of Busey Bank in Champaign, Illinois, illustrated the point well. He said, "If you eat a high-fat diet, smoke, or live a sedentary lifestyle for forty years and you develop heart disease at age sixty-five, your cardiologist can offer help in the form of drugs, surgery, and behavior changes. Yet, if you come to me at age sixty-five without having saved any money, without having taken advantage of forty years of compound interest, there is not much I can do for you. If only at age seven you had saved eighty-six cents a day (at 10 percent interest), by age sixty-five you'd have over a million dollars."

OK. So you probably aren't seven years old. At age thirty, if you save $8.60 per day you'd be a millionaire by age sixty-five. Even at the age of forty, a mere $21 daily donation will give you a six-figure bank account at retirement. Not a bad microaction.

## Connect with Microactions

I really have no clue why microactions work so well. Usually the tinier and the seemingly less useful the movement is, the more it works in getting us past our resistance. Sara Sorensen wrote to me about her resolution (and teeny, tiny step) to accept her adult daughter's way of doing things when she came for a visit. She avoided creating a tense (and disconnected) situation by simply biting her tongue. She said, "I remember how irritated I would become when my own mother criticized the way I opened cans. The microaction of keeping my mouth shut has made my daughter's vacation more enjoyable for both of us."

Microactions can work in any field. My husband uses them with the high school students he counsels. Seventeen-year-olds have a thousand ingenious reasons why they have not yet applied for college admission. Instead of harping on them to fill out the application and warning them of the dire consequences if they fail to act in time, he asks them to bring in a postage stamp. He instructs them first to lick the stamp (they roll their eyes) and then place it on an addressed envelope in his presence. He reminds them that everyone who has graduated from college first put a stamp on an envelope and mailed in the application. The kids think his advice is so stupid they mail in the forms. What else are they going to do with the stamped envelope?

You know what your life-balance barriers are and what will help. You know it is hard to make yourself do the "right thing." You may even be sick and tired of thinking about doing the right thing. So outthink yourself. Try something really ludicrous. One man told me he hated to mow the lawn. His wife nagged and the neighbors frowned. He decided to look out the window at the grass, shake his head in disgust, and say, "Tsk, tsk, tsk." He did it every day for a week. He said after a week of daily head shakes, the long grass started to bother even him and he couldn't wait to mow!

And then there is flossing. Do you floss twice a day every day? If we all did, there wouldn't be a dentist office on every corner. But really, why in the world won't we floss daily? We know it will help keep our teeth from falling out. Yet no one says, "I don't floss because I really don't mind being toothless from periodontal disease in a few years." Flossing is not expensive, time-consuming, painful, embarrassing, or exhausting. It has the technical difficulty of zero. One of my graduate students said her microaction would be to just hold the floss. Don't laugh. She's probably flossing right now.

## Music to My Ears

I've heard from hundreds of people who now swear by microactions. Nina Rubinelli wrote, "Sometimes my lists become overwhelming. The too-much-to-do-too-little-time anxiety turns into procrastination. As you predicted, the microactions sometimes seem so ridiculous that we have to laugh at ourselves and go on to complete the task. With big jobs, the smaller steps make the process easier."

Use microactions to put more connections in your life. Ask yourself, "What change do I want to make? What's my barrier? What microaction could I use to move from 'gonna do' to 'follow through'?"

Good luck!

## THE NEW SOLUTION:
## MICROACTIONS

*When we can't keep up, we have a choice. We can:*

| DISCONNECT | CONNECT |
|---|---|
| **Be the worst procrastinator** | **Be the best microactor** |
| I'll save money as soon as I get all my bills paid off. | I'll put $2.67 a week in the jar on my dresser. |
| **Take great gulps and fail** | **Take teeny, tiny steps and succeed** |
| The change is so big—where would I start? | What would have to happen first to make this change? |
| **Give lip service** | **Give real service** |
| My family comes first and as soon as I get this promotion I'll have time for them. | How can I stay connected with my family while I work for this promotion? |

This is not a book on how to do more. It is a book on how to do what you want to do. We can get closer to what we want, we can shorten that distance between our lips and our lives, by nudging ourselves gently along with microactions. As Mikey's brothers told him in the famous cereal commercial, "Try it, you'll like it."

## MICROACTIONS

1. Make a list of your top three life-balance challenges.
   For example:
   a. I can't seem to find the time or motivation to exercise.
   b. I need to improve my relationship with my spouse.
   c. I don't save enough money.

2.  Under each one, identify *who* (besides you) and *what* this challenge affects. For instance, if getting more exercise is one of the challenges you listed, who else does this affect? Will your spouse be willing to baby-sit while you go to the gym? Will you miss breakfast with the family while you go for a run in the morning? Could your family benefit because you will be healthier and better able to care for them? Would more energy allow you to better meet your day-to-day obligations at work?

3.  List people or things that could help you meet your challenges. Perhaps you want to start a monthly savings plan. Does your employer offer an automatic deposit program for a savings account? Have you written a budget? Have you met with your banker or credit adviser to consolidate loans? Is there a trusted friend who can guide you? Can you start tracking your expenses in a notebook?

4.  Write down what you have tried that didn't work. (Here I list things like hollering at the kids to pick up their toys, buying a dress one size too small, and asking my brother for a loan.)

5.  List actions that have had some success in the past. Perhaps you and your spouse had a weekly date night that was very successful but then you changed jobs and the dates went by the wayside. Is it time to give date night another try? Is there something you both enjoy doing? What did you used to do for fun?

6.  Write down one microaction for each challenge you have listed under number 1—the smaller and sillier the better.

7.  Go take a nap. You will want to be rested for all the wonderful things that will happen to you after you finish this book.

## IN REAL LIFE

Dear Mary,

It was very "akamai" ("smart" in Hawaiian) of you to have us verbalize and commit to our microactions. First, I committed to begin a walking program the very next day. I woke up that day and thought to myself, "Oh, it's Friday, I'll just start on Monday." Since I made the promise aloud to others ("I will start a walking program tomorrow morning"), I walked three miles that morning and kept it up all summer. As the saying goes, "Just do it!" Second, I promised to read one chapter of my new graphic organizer book and before I knew it, I had finished the entire book. We were to commit to five of our ten microactions in a month, but once I got started, I accomplished all ten!

Sincerely,

Theresa Lynn Johnson

Grade 5 teacher

Kailua, Oahu

# CHAPTER 4

# Tap into Your Passion

*Do not worry about what the world wants of you.
Worry about what makes you come alive, because
what the world needs is people who are more alive.*
—Dr. Lawrence LeShan

"As soon as I get my work done at the office . . . the garage cleaned . . . all the bills paid . . . the laundry finished . . . then I'll do what I really enjoy." The old solution to life balance was to give up some or all of our passions to get everything done first. Frankly, it often worked. But it doesn't work that way anymore. There is always one (or fifty-six) more things to do. Many people have been on the treadmill for so long they have convinced themselves they have no time for what they truly enjoy, that it is not even a realistic goal for which to strive. They reason, if I can't get everything done —if I can't keep up as it is, surely I can't afford the time or the luxury of engaging in my passions.

The connection solution proposes just the opposite. In this fast-paced world, we don't have the luxury of *not* putting a skip in our step. Success is going to require all the zest for life we can muster. Ralph Waldo Emerson said, "We are always getting ready to live but never living." Staying in balance is not worth the effort if we feel no excitement for life. Fortunately, if we tap into our passions, we connect with ourselves, and when we do that, our lives have a way of coming into balance.

## A Bird in a Cage Will Forget How to Sing

When I was thirty-six years old, I didn't have much passion in my life. I was the director of the Hypertension Research Center, I had three children, ages nine, six, and three, and I helped take care of my eighty-year-old widowed mother-in-law. I had totally bought into the superwoman role, and needless to say, I was exhausted. My greatest challenge in life was to keep the laundry from piling to the ceiling. My focus was not on living my passion, but rather on just getting enough done each day so I could start doing it all over again. One day I woke up and discovered I could not go on like that anymore. I made a very serious decision to put some passion into my life. You, too, may have come to a crossroads and realized you were not living your dream. Drastic times call for drastic measures.

So I joined a men's basketball league. Now don't laugh! I want you to know there were four (count them, *four*) *consecutive* games in which I scored a basket—which I lovingly referred to as "the streak." It was the most fun I had had in years. I felt alive and unafraid.

About the same time my forty-year-old husband started a fifties rock band. Our friends thought we had just gone off the cliff. I could hear them silently lament, "Those LoVerdes— they seemed like such *nice, normal* people!"

My female friends were really up in arms about my husband's new band. "But it isn't fair," they insisted. "You work all week and then you sit home with three kids on a Saturday night while he is out somewhere playing his guitar. It's just not right!"

They had a point. I could have insisted that he stay home and, quite frankly, he would have. He loves me and had I complained, he would have given up the band. But what would I have? I'd have a man sitting in my living room on a Saturday night who wants to be playing a guitar in a honky-tonk. That is not a prize! But you see, this way, at two o'clock in the morning, crawling into bed with me is a man who *thinks* he's Michael Bolton!

One of the nicest gifts we can give the person we're sharing our lives with is the support and time to pursue his/her passion —even if we don't fully understand it. Do you know what your mate or best friend is passionate about? Do you help him or her stay in love with life? Or has life deteriorated into a list of never-ending chores?

## "To Do or Not To Do"

When we get married, we say "I do" but then, for some rea-son, we . . . *don't!* Didn't we initially make a commitment to help each other live life to its fullest? Instead of "I do," we make a long "I don't" list. We say, "I don't do this and I don't do that—well, you know, I'm *married.*" Let's face it. There are only a few items that *must* appear on the "I don't" list. I think we should make our "I do" list much longer than our "I don't" list. It's almost as if we say, "I won't do anything I really like to do and that will prove I love you, and then you don't do anything you really like to do and that will prove you love me, and in about fifteen years, not only will we be two of the most miserable people in the world, we'll be two of the most boring people in the world."

But what if you're sharing your life with someone who

doesn't share your passions and interests? How do you stay in love with someone who's incredibly boring? And miserable? And what if *you're* the one who's incredibly boring and miserable?

Good questions. My audiences tell me they have solved the problem of mismatched passions in three ways.

## 1. If you can't beat 'em, join 'em.

One nurse told me of her husband's passion for collecting old war memorabilia. It was not exactly her cup of tea. Still, she went along nearly every weekend, sitting in the corner of the show and reading a book. One day her husband bought her an old medical tool used in the war. She said, "As an OR nurse, it was fascinating to me. All of a sudden I loved it. Now we hunt together and he delights in finding me something for my collection and I do the same for him." Many couples report they solve their dilemma by simply giving it a try.

## 2. I will go with you if you will go with me.

Remember in kindergarten when the teacher taught us that annoying habit of taking turns? It still works. If you are committed to helping each other live life to the fullest you may decide to go bird-watching on the even days and skeet-shooting on the odd. The important part is not to keep score, but rather enjoy the fact that you are not cleaning out the car.

## 3. I love you but . . .

Right before I got married, my husband-to-be bought a water-ski boat. Talk about a passion! With his enthusiasm for his new purchase (and, I perceived, not for our wedding), I felt left out. He reassured me I was first in his life when he said, "I love you more than the boat . . . but don't ever test me." In twenty years I never have. We have had several boats and countless boating adventures and he would not be the same man without his life at sea. We have spent several children's college tuitions on boats, storage, equipment, repairs, trips, magazine subscriptions, insurance, water toys, and trips to the emergency room and subsequent surgeons. I like the boat and we go together often but I will never be as crazy about his passion as he is. He loves me and he loves his boat.

On the other hand, I can look at antique furniture for days. I don't usually buy, just look. This drives him crazy. And it makes me crazy when I have just started hunting and he has seen all the "old junk" he can stand. So I go alone. We like it that way. I love him because he supports my passion . . . I love him most when he is happy and so am I.

If sitting in a boat, watching the depth finder, and baiting hooks sounds like torture, if hiding in the duck blind at dawn seems preposterous, or if the last thing you'd ever say is, "Gee, honey, I'd love to go to the mall. Can I hold your purse while you shop?" then maybe it is time to invoke the "I love you but . . ." strategy. Golf widows or widowers know this one best. If you can golf together, great. But what if the golf fanatic is paired with a partner who can throw it farther than drive it? Then it is time to sit down and find out how you can both tap into your passions and *still stay connected.* Remember, it is when we are feeling disconnected that we hurt most. Be reasonable and flexible and don't assume being passionate about some-thing else means your special one is less passionate about you. It is not a contest.

## It's Not What You Think

People who get a kick out of life reject the myths of passion.

Myth #1: Passion is exuberance.

Not true. Passion may be exuberant but not necessarily so. For me, when I am excited about something, the joy just bubbles to the top. That's me. Perhaps that's you, too. But we all know people who say with a flat affect in a dull monotone, "That was the most exciting thing that has ever happened to me in my whole life." And they mean it! Despite their lack of outward expression, inside they are feeling just what I am. Get passionate about something and don't worry if the exuberance is inside or out.

Myth #2: We have to be good at it to
be passionate about it.

Nope. This little secret comes as a big revelation to many of us, especially we baby boomers, who grew up believing that not only did we have to be good at it, we had to be *the best* at it, or we couldn't really be passionate about it. We believed it was a waste of our time if we didn't really excel at it. I say, "Horsefeathers!"

You don't have to necessarily be any good at it. It just has to ring your bell. My basketball league is a good case in point. I had played in high school and college but it had been fifteen years and three babies ago that I played in a Real Basketball Game. I was understandably a little nervous. In addition to my long sabbatical from the sport, I was playing with men—very competitive macho men who did not really comprehend that this was a Thursday night league game. In their minds, this was the NBA. You can imagine my embarrassment when, the first time down the court, in my very first game, the rebound hit me on top of the head! It didn't matter, though; I was having the time of my life.

I hate to admit this in print, but my husband is not a particularly talented musician. The Father of Rhythm he's not. But what he lacks in rhythm, he makes up for in enthusiasm. What he really loves to do is dance. So at all his gigs he would ask the women to dance while the band played on. The women loved it (he did too!) and their parties were always lots of fun. He used this tactic so often that when he would come home at night, I'd say, "So did you actually plug your guitar in tonight?" And when the band members described him they would say, "As a guitarist, that Joe is a really really good . . . dancer." His ineptness as a musician did not get in the way of his yearning to be a rock star.

> Myth #3: I have to choose an exciting topic or
> activity or something out of the ordinary.

False. I am not suggesting you become a professional bungee jumper. Maybe you like to crochet, hike, or read. Maybe you're a fly fisherman, an avid sailor, or a cook or gardener. It could be the relationship you have with your God that fills you with passion. Do whatever floats your boat, puts the cha-cha into your step, or satisfies your longing. Balance will follow.

In one of my seminars I asked the participants to share what they were passionate about. Eva Huskey, a lovely woman in her sixties, stood up and eloquently, in a thick accent, said, "I am passionate about my children and grandchildren. I spend as much time as I can with them. I am also excited about oil painting. I paint every chance I get. However, I am most passionate about patriotism. I love this country. I grew up in Hitler's Germany and then lived under Russian occupation. In 1951 an East German border guard helped me escape to West Germany, where I met my future husband, who took me to the United States. I thank God every day for the freedom I have found. I know that you have problems here. But you do not really understand how wonderful it is to live in a country that guarantees the inalienable right to life, liberty, and the pursuit of happiness. I am very passionate about the patriotism I feel for this wonderful nation."

There wasn't a dry eye in the room. We were all moved by the love Eva expressed and we went away with a new understanding of what passion meant.

## But What If I Am Passionate About Work?

Good for you. Someone once said, "Love what you do and you will never work a day in your life." Loving your work is a blessing, not a curse. What gets us into trouble is when we let work disconnect us from those we love. If we leave our significant others with empty buckets and then go to work to fill up our own, we can expect to be out of balance.

I spoke to the Rubber Manufacturers Association and received a letter from one of the CEOs. He wrote, "My wife and I talked about my passion for work for three hours after your program. Do you always cause this much trouble?"

I hope so. My heartfelt wish is for you to talk with your loved one about work and life and find ways to help each other live happily ever after.

## Passionate? Who, Me?

Curiously, many people have confided to me that they believe they are not supposed to be passionate or feel they don't deserve it. Brenda Bresie wrote, "My friends and I are still talking about finding that passion. However, I think the hardest part is giving ourselves permission."

Permission is a common theme that emerges whenever my audiences discuss passion. Is it our Puritan work ethic, our drive for perfection, or ill-placed guilt that keeps us from throwing caution to the wind?

I believe humans inherently need passion. Peter Falk said, "I guess everyone wants two things. People want one foot where they feel safe and secure. They want to know what the future holds. But everyone has a part of them that would like to be wild, unpredictable—and different. An original."

It is the "original" part that gives us the spark we need to be happy. So why do we need permission? Why can't we accept that we are powerful and passionate creatures who can give in to the wild side once in a while? Doing so might even give others permission to do the same.

The bottom line: You do not need any more permission to be passionate about life. You were given permission when you took your first breath. After all, who are you *not* to be passionate?

## But How Do I Find the Time?

Have you ever noticed that when something is really important you somehow find the time? Make passion a priority. One way to free up some time is to eliminate distractions.

I stopped cooking. Not that I was exactly slaving in the kitchen for hours preparing exotic meals. I did, however, have this false impression that I cooked. As it turns out, "cooking" was a term I used loosely. I didn't realize how loosely until my daughter pointed it out to me.

Upon returning from a trip to Iowa to visit Grandma and Grandpa (where she insisted they have "real meals"), Emily asked me to tell her a story about my childhood.

I told her about watching my parents dress chickens. I gave her all the gory details. (There is a reason we describe a hysterical person as "running around like a chicken with his head cut off.")

I loved telling her the story. "And then we'd pluck off all the feathers to make pillows. Grandma knew how to cut the chicken up in a special way and on Sunday she'd fry the chickens for a big dinner after church."

I knew the story would impress her. She is a remarkably insightful, sensitive child and I was ready for her philosophical questions about animal rights, etc. With her eyes big as saucers she exclaimed, "You can . . . FRY . . . chicken?"

Well, you know, she'd never seen anyone do it at my house. The Colonel did all our frying. Emily had no idea the common man could do it.

I realized I am not jazzed about cooking. Never have been. Never will be. Getting rid of this distraction could free me up to pursue what I truly enjoy. I love the family to have dinner together, but surely there is someone besides me who can prepare meals.

It turns out there are lots of volunteers. I discovered Chinese takeout can be delivered. Who woulda guessed? I call it Carton Cuisine. My husband is a very good cook (if you like spaghetti every night) and my new motto is, "Pizza: the pot roast of the nineties."

OK. So my diet is not quite that bad. But I have resigned

myself to the fact that I am more passionate about decorating the kitchen than I am about using the oven. And if I do say so myself, my interior designing is "tasteful."

The year I remodeled the kitchen my brother Bob asked me what I wanted for Christmas. I told him I wanted a white coffeemaker.

He said, "I am not familiar with that brand."

I replied, "I don't care what brand you get. I don't even make coffee. It just needs to be white so it'll go with the wallpaper."

He laughed. "You really don't cook, do you?"

The coffeemaker matched perfectly.

What about you? Could you free up some time and refocus your energies into something that really makes you lick your chops? What "distractions" could you delegate or eliminate?

## What If I Don't Know What I Am Passionate About?

Be patient. You'll find out once you give it to your subconscious to figure out. It may not be a hobby or sport. Maybe you are passionate about variety and you will never stick to just one thing. What turns us on will change. I don't play much basketball anymore. It is a rough-and-tumble sport and at age forty-four, I like my teeth right where they are. My love for basketball is now redirected into weight lifting.

## Passion Can Balance Your Life—and Save It

I believe that tapping into your passion will solve many of your life-balance problems. I know it will dramatically improve your relationships if you help your loved ones to express their delight. Still, as vital as all these reasons are, another benefit looms even larger. Through psychoneuroimmunology we know being passionate will boost your immune system. We can scientifically measure what happens to your T cells when you're exhilarated.

Over forty years ago Lawrence LeShan, a clinical psychologist and the godfather of the mind-body movement, began investigating the association between passion and the immune system in pioneering work with cancer patients. He selected the patients labeled "hopeless" because he did not know if his therapy would work, and ethically he did not want to take patients away from traditional therapy. He worked with these so-called hopeless patients one-on-one and asked them, "What are you passionate about?" Together they explored the question and worked out ways to get some excitement into their lives.

Lawrence LeShan's patients, using techniques described in the books *You Can Fight for Your Life* and *Cancer as a Turning Point*, have an unusually high rate of remission (nearly 50 percent according to LeShan). Therapists trained in these techniques get similar results. Dr. LeShan clarified, "Bad thoughts don't cause cancer and good thoughts can't cure it. That's nonsense." Instead, he believes we can awaken our immune system to function on a higher level by replacing complacency with gusto. We send a message to our immune system, "Hey! I've got things to live for. Get going!"

Dr. LeShan tells a wonderful story about one of his patients, Pedro, a twenty-year-old Hispanic man, who had been a gang member in the South Bronx since age nine. At age sixteen he reached the highest position, "warlord." Having been deserted by his father at an early age, he finally felt that he had come into his own and that the gang was where he belonged. As with many gangs, his group eventually broke up. Some of his brothers went to jail; some died; others joined the army, got married, or moved away. Left alone on the streets, he was devastated, and about a year later, he developed Hodgkin's disease at a time when we could not cure it. The medical community threw up their hands and told Pedro to go home and die. He started working with Lawrence LeShan and Lawrence asked, "What thrills you in life?"

The man replied, "What I really like is being a gang leader."

"Well," Dr. LeShan said, "You can't be a gang leader. But tell me, what is it *about* being the warlord that you love so much?"

The man's eyes lit up and he said, "What I love is the exhilaration of going into the heat of the battle with my brothers behind me, knowing that each of them would be willing to lay their lives down for one another. And in between times, I love the camaraderie of just laying around, playing cards, and drinking beer."

Lawrence LeShan is such a smart man. He said, "Then I suggest you get an education and become a fireman. Because, you see, firemen go into the heat of the battle with their brothers behind them knowing that each of them would be willing to lay their lives down for one another." (And in between times, they lay around and play cards and make pancakes.)

That is precisely what the man did, and he is still alive today.

If tapping into passion can put deadly cancers into remission, just think what it could do to help you connect with yourself. Sink your teeth into something.

## So What Do I Do Now?

Norman Vincent Peale says, "Throw your heart over the bar and your body will follow." Merilee Light from Allina Health

System in Minneapolis followed his advice. She called me to say, "After your talk I couldn't stop thinking about that passion thing. I walked around the lake, thinking, 'What am I passionate about?' Finally it dawned on me. Water! I have always been drawn to water. So I want you to know I have scheduled a vacation in Aruba and signed up for windsurfing lessons. I can't begin to tell you how this has changed my life."

I am not surprised. I hear it all the time. Another woman wrote to me, "Your discussion about tapping into passion really hit home. I realized it had been so long since I felt really passionate about anything that I'd forgotten what it was! I suppose I need to do some soul searching."

Don't we all.

## THE NEW SOLUTION:
## PASSION

*When we can't keep up, we have a choice. We can:*

| DISCONNECT | CONNECT |
|---|---|
| **Be boring** | **Be brand new** |
| I am always tired. If only I could get everything done. | I have always wanted to try square dancing. I could take a class Thursday nights. |
| **Make an "I don't" list** | **Make an "I do" list** |
| I can't sign up for that golf tournament. My wife would have a fit. | Life is short. "Honey, let's talk about how we can *both* spice up our lives." |
| **Get extinguished** | **Get excited** |
| I feel depressed a lot. My life is just "Hi ho, off to work I go." | I can give myself permission to have a whole life. |

You can decide your life is just too busy already and the last thing you need is something else to do. After all, you have enough trouble getting the work done as it is. You can conclude that since you don't get to live your dreams, your loved one shouldn't expect to live his or hers either.

Or . . . you can ask, "What am I passionate about? When was the last time something fanned my flame? If I know what I am excited about, what is holding me back? What can I do to support my spouse or loved ones in pursuing their dreams?"

## MICROACTIONS

1.  Make a sign with this quote by Nicholas Murray Butler: "Many people's tombstones should read, 'Died at 30. Buried at 60.' " Put it somewhere so you'll read it everyday. Then make sure it doesn't apply to you.
2.  Ask your significant other or friends what they are passionate about.
3.  Make a list of things you love to do. See any trends?
4.  Write out a list of activities that occupy your day (for example, ironing shirts, commuting, standing in line, reading e-mail, etc.) and identify some that, if eliminated or delegated away, would leave you more time for your passions.
5.  Sit in on an Internet chat room discussion of your favorite topic.
6.  Buy something having to do with the activity you'd like to try. Want to go camping? Buy a thermos, a sleeping bag, or a tent. You'll feel silly owning a brand new one and then never using it. You'll have to go camping!
7.  Just go do it! What are you waiting for?

## IN REAL LIFE

Dear Mary,

After hearing you speak at the Bodylife England Conference I wanted to tell you why your message touched me so. Three years ago at the age of twenty-seven I had a mastectomy, with an excellent prognosis and no risk factors. The future looked great. Unfortunately in July, a number of secondaries were detected and I am presently on hormone treatment pending test results on my original tumour. Despite the medical profession's attempts to paint a fairly somber picture I have remained positive and passionate about the future. Indeed it is often me who keeps both my friends and family from feeling low about my cancer. Naturally when I heard you recite research into the beneficial effects of positive attitude on terminal cancer patients, I was intrigued. Can I therefore ask you for relevant references? It may even be a good idea to give a copy to my consultant!!!!

However, your wrap-up speech at the end of the conference did more than just give me a research reference. It reminded me of the principles by which I try to live my life. At a time when my life is not quite going to plan you helped to refocus me on what is important. Indeed, I started my five positive things that very night and I sent two thank-you cards to people who have greatly supported me recently.

Thank you once again for reminding me of what is really important in life and can I say that when it comes to being passionate and having fun I have never had more than I am having right now.

Kind regards,

Maddie Cropper

Great Britain

Two years later I received this letter from Maddie.

Dear Mary,

Your letter finds me well and looking forward to a family Christmas. Professionally, 1998 looks to be an exciting year for my company and in turn it may present some opportunities for me, God willing.

On the health front I am well although the last two years have been a challenge—including two four-month courses of chemo and radiotherapy. However, I do seem to be bouncing back although I'm sure that without my friends, family, and colleagues' support it would have been more difficult.

Fortunately, I have continued working through treatment and have relative "normality" in my life. Indeed, I am optimistic for 1998 and the possible career options I may have. In many ways my illness has put me in touch with an inner strength and passion I never knew I had, which has helped me to find peace.

I wish you and your family well and will write more in the New Year.

Regards,

Maddie

# PART II

## *Connecting* with Your Family

# CHAPTER 5

# Marriage and Romance: No, It's Not an Oxymoron

Why it's hard to keep your marriage one long, heavenly, romantic dream.

> Almost no one is foolish enough to imagine that he automatically deserves great success in any field of activity; yet almost everyone believes that he automatically deserves success in marriage.
>
> —*Sydney J. Harris*

Consider these words:

Prenuptial agreement, significant other, musk oil, Heidi Fleiss, same-sex marriages, Victoria's Secret, and the Miracle Bra.

Romance doesn't seem to be as easy as it once was. Rules, expectations, and norms have changed. What hasn't changed is the power romance has to connect us.

Romance is a broad concept. Maybe you long to re-create the steamy scenes on the daytime drama *The Bold and the Beautiful.* You may want to be romantic with someone you are sharing your life with. You can also put romance into your life in many ways—even if you are "between partners." You can get the *sense* of romance through art, literature, travel, lace, theater, antiques, music—living vicariously is quite all right!

However you choose to include romance, it will take some planning. Our fast-paced "fill it to the max" life doesn't readily lend itself to romantic novels, long candlelit baths, walks in the moonlight, or love letters—unless you do some scheming. Don't believe the myth that if you have to schedule it, you take away all the fun and mystique. You only lose the fun and mystique if nothing happens, and chances are nothing will happen unless you prepare for it.

## 1001 Ways to Keep Your Lover

When I suggest to people that romance will balance their lives I get two excuses. The first is, "Sure, I'd like to be more romantic, but I can't ever think of anything." Well, if that is your excuse, too, your worries are over. "It" has already been thought of! Gregory Godek wrote a wonderful book entitled *1001 Ways to Be Romantic* (Sourcebooks, 1995). He has a sequel called *1001 More Ways to Be Romantic* (Sourcebooks, 1995). That is 2002 ideas—if you need more than that please call me and I will give you another one. (One woman in my audience shouted out, "If you need more than 2002 please call *me!*") Greg's book is especially helpful for busy people because you don't have to actually *read* it. Just open it to any page.

---

HONEY, Tonight It's Number 599!*

Here are some of my favorites:

#588: "Guys: On your wedding anniversary, re-create her wedding bouquet. (If this doesn't bring tears to her eyes, divorce her.) Since you may not know a chrysanthemum from poison ivy, show one of your wedding photos to your florist."

#694: "Fake a power outage at home. (Loosen the fuses or throw the breaker switches.) Get out the candles. Then try to think of *something* to do."

#697: "Slow dance at a restaurant—*when there's no music playing.* (When one man did this with his girlfriend, he reported that they were applauded by the other patrons, and given a complimentary bottle of champagne by the management!)"

#889: "Write your own version of Elizabeth Barrett Browning's famous poem . . . '*How do I love thee, let me count the ways . . .*' "

#904: "Arrange with an airline steward or stewardess to have a gift or flower delivered to her (or him) right after the flight is airborne."

(*Courtesy of Gregory Godek.)

---

### Secret Admirers

I spoke to a delightful audience in Minneapolis last year. After my introductory remarks on romance, I asked them to pair up and tell each other the last romantic thing they had done. The entire audience looked at their shoes.

I said, "Maybe you didn't understand me. Just pair up and describe the last romantic gesture you made." Again they stared at their shoes. Finally I shouted, "MOVE!" Groaning, each person found a partner and, with some reluctance, they discussed romance. I then invited them to share their ideas with the whole group. Their intense interest in the tops of their shoes reappeared. I just stood there waiting.

Out of the corner of my eye, I saw a man stretching, scratching his head, and then, with trepidation, slowly raising his hand. At that point I was willing to call on anybody who moved. "Yes, sir, please tell us. What was the last romantic thing you did?"

"Well," he said shyly, "I bought a romantic card, signed it Your Secret Admirer, and sent it to my wife at her office."

The whole audience cooed, "Ahhhhhhhhhhhh."

He shook his head. "When my wife read it, she called me at my office—hysterical. She thought she'd received a card from a stalker!"

I didn't quite know what to say. Finally I stammered, "Gosh, sir, that is unfortunate. And what did you learn from this?"

He scratched his head again and grinned. "I learned that perhaps it's time to step up the frequency of those cards if, after twenty years, my wife doesn't even recognize my hand-writing!"

When was the last time you sent a romantic card? When was the last time you received one?

## The Highlight of His Day

My heart was warmed by a very attractive woman in her fifties who spoke to me after my program in Ohio.

"That story about sending cards really hit home. Last year my husband had a stroke. I work all day and then I go home and care for him all night. It is very difficult for both of us. And you know what? I realized today that I haven't sent him a romantic card since he suffered his stroke. Checking the mail every day is one of his only highlights. I just decided my new ritual will be to send him a romantic card every week."

Indeed. Perhaps it is time for all of us to step up the frequency of those cards.

## And Baby Makes Three

I met a charming man on a plane one day. As often happens, when I told him my line of business, we began a discussion of his life-balance concerns. He and his wife were both successful professionals in their thirties and had a beautiful six-month-old baby. The man had the typical and legitimate issues: not enough time to go around, a struggle with the new and vague division of labor, and feelings of being second to the needs of the child. He also expressed dismay at their infrequent and disappointing sex life. He said he and his wife had quarreled before he left. She was angry because his life seemed to go on as usual and she was left with all the child care duties, her job, the housework, etc.

I agreed that his feelings were justified. The transition from couple to parents is a rocky road for most. Both the man and the woman have major adjustments.

"Well," I began, "since you have confided in me, may I ask some questions? Is your wife nursing?"

"Yes. And she pumps her breasts constantly to freeze enough

milk for the baby when she is at work. I told her I would do sit-ups while she pumped but I couldn't keep up! It is a very time-consuming activity."

I smiled. "Did you know that when a woman is breast-feeding a hormone called prolactin is secreted from the pituitary? This regulates milk production. Because it lowers estrogen levels, prolactin can also nip a woman's sex drive in the bud. This is nature's way. A breast-feeding woman probably doesn't want to get pregnant. A suppressed libido is Mother Nature's contribution to the cause. Many nursing mothers who don't understand this secretly worry that their sex drive is lost forever. It's important to know that after she weans your child (and she gets some sleep), her interest will most likely return. She needs your support.

"In addition, she's had a major body image change. Imagine if one of your favorite anatomical parts had to enlarge to ten times its normal size and then open up to let the baby out! Imagine if you were now seen at work as being less valuable because you have child-care issues. Imagine if you were uncertain about whether your spouse still found you attractive.

"I don't want to be a buttinski . . . but since *you* brought it up . . . maybe what she wants to hear is simply that you recognize all the efforts she has made and is continuing to make to create a wonderful family for both of you. Maybe you could send her a romantic card and make a long list of all these things and say thanks. Maybe you could remind her that you still find her attractive and you look forward to romantic times with her. It's just a thought."

We went back to our books and the rest of the flight was silent. As we were deplaning he turned to me and said, "Thanks a lot for the information on prolactin. I'm relieved to know someday we will be back to our old selves. I have some time before I make my next flight. I'm going to buy her a romantic card right now."

Being romantic is simple. Sometimes just understanding and saying so is all that is needed. Lose the excuse that you can't think of anything.

---

### THE LOVE BEEPER

Romance is one of the few things in life that doesn't have to cost money. One woman said that she created a list of codes for her husband. She calls his pager and puts in the codes daily:

1111 = I love you.

2222 = Thinking about you.

3333 = Can't wait to see you.

4444 = Hi Handsome!

5555 = Testimony! Call me!

She said sometimes she puts in a code, then hangs up and keeps calling back. "I keep him vibrating for five minutes!"

---

## Stud Muffins and Hot Mamas

The second excuse I hear is, "You know, in my day I was quite a lady's man (romantic soul, hot number, big stud, etc.) and I would like to be romantic. But what with my job and commuting, the kids and the carpooling, I just don't have enough time."

It is said that a picture is worth a thousand words:

**For Better or For Worse®**                              **by Lynn Johnston**

Yes, we are all busy. But let's make a commitment not to be *so* busy that we turn our backs on romance.

## It's Been a Long Time

What if it has been quite a while between romantic gestures? Won't it seem awkward to just start being romantic? What if my diaphragm has cobwebs? Won't my spouse think I've gone off the deep end—or worse?

If that is your concern, you might be surprised. Many happy couples who have simply gotten out of the habit have rekindled their love for each other with just a simple gesture. It's kind of like riding a bicycle. Even if it has been a long time, once you start, it all seems to come back to you.

One of my audience members said this was her experience. This determined woman decided to add some romance to her marriage with a daily voice message to her husband. "The first day I left a little 'I love you' message on his work voice mail. My husband laughed. I left another one the next day. My husband said, 'Why are you doing this?' The third day I left another one. He laughed again. So I quit. On the fourth day he called me and said, 'Hey! Where's my message?' "

Try a little romance. It can't hurt.

### THE RADIATION FROM TELEVISION MAKES US IMPOTENT AND FRIGID

OK. That's not true. But now that I have your attention, let me suggest that a TV in the bedroom is worse than a cold shower when it comes to romance and good sex. First of all, sleep experts tell us that there are only two things we should do in bed. Sleep is one of them. Watching television is not the other one! Get the TV out of there! Why don't I have a TV in our bedroom? Because I don't want to have to *compete* with the television, that's why. I'd have to be funnier than David Letterman, sexier than the babes on *Baywatch,* and more exciting than the Play of the Week on ESPN. Can't you just see me—naming the Top Ten Reasons We Should Make Love, wearing a low-cut, high-rise life guard swimming suit, and making a diving catch off the end of the bed—all in an effort to get his attention? After twenty years of marriage, I don't need that kind of pressure—if you know what I mean.

What? You say the TV has been in the bedroom forever and you fear removing it would cause civil war? Or that you really like watching a little TV to help you unwind? Then I suggest you just turn it off one night a week, or thirty minutes earlier in the evening (fifteen minutes earlier is enough for some of us). Change your routine a little bit, cut down on the distractions, and just see what happens.

## Happily Ever After?
"All marriages are happy. It's the living together
afterward that causes all the trouble."
(Raymond Hull)

Let's face it. Everybody's marriage has "living together after-ward" problems. Money, in-laws, kids, differences over religion or sex, division of labor issues—not to mention that the person you married years ago had the audacity to change! Keeping our marriage *together*, much less romantic, is nearly "mission impossible" some days. Sometimes divorce is the logical answer. Still, for most of us, a happy relationship heads the list of things we need to make our lives balanced.

Few studies have been done on what makes a marriage happy. I guess it is easier to study what is wrong with something than what is right. That doesn't mean there aren't any really good marriages. Despite the fact that one in two unions end in divorce, I believe long, loving, lasting marriages are possible.

When researchers survey Americans about what they need most to have a happy life, a good marriage heads the list. Friends, jobs, and money are distant cousins.

So, if for most of us marriage comes first, how can we improve it and thereby enhance the quality of our lives?

Early in our marriage my husband, Joe, and I devised three rules to live by.

1.  We must believe we belong with each other.
Tattoo on your foreheads (invisible ink is OK) "We belong together." (This is different than we belong *to* each other.) You must see yourself as a unit, a whole, a complete set. Your union

doesn't require anyone else. This means you see yourself as separate from your other families.

For wedding presents, I always give a money gift, inviting the new couple to buy something that signifies their new family. One couple bought a beautiful Santa and sleigh for Christmas, their way of saying, "This is how the new Mr. and Mrs. Hood family decorate for the Christmas holidays."

Another woman told me when she and her husband got married they had a major blowout with his mother over how to celebrate birthdays. His family always dined with their large extended family on birthdays. She said she fell in love with him all over again when her husband informed his mother he would be taking his wife out for a romantic dinner on her birthday because "that's how *our* family celebrates birthdays."

Have you made it clear to your other families that *your* family is numero uno? I am not suggesting you refuse to give them your address (although in some cases . . .). And I suppose your brother will wonder why he can't have your unlisted telephone number. A happy medium will go a long way toward maintaining a happy marriage. Make sure you belong first and foremost *with* each other.

## Enter Cutie Pie

This unity also applies when the little ankle-biters come along. It's often said the best thing parents can do for kids is to love their spouse. When the baby comes, it's not that we stop loving our mate. We just focus so much of our energy on the darling interloper that our marriage sometimes takes a backseat. Dave Barry believes that when a baby is born, Mother Nature causes both parents to secrete vast quantities of IQ-reduction hormones, so that "the parents are just smart enough to feed and change the baby but dumb enough to be highly amused if the baby inadvertently makes a noise such as gwooooossshh." About the time we recover from the temporary hormonal imbalance, we are hit with a host of distractions like tuba lessons, chicken pox, debate club, broken arms, dance recitals, ball practices, homework, and broken hearts. It's not easy, but if our marriage is to flourish, we must carve out some time. This means it is necessary to tell the kids no and your lover yes. We owe this not only to ourselves, but to our children. How will they learn how to be happily married if we don't model it for them? How will they know it takes time to make a relationship work if we don't show them how? How will they know who is in charge of the remote control?

Are you lovers first and parents second? Do you make time for your marriage?

## When the Going Gets Tough

You must also be a single force when crisis hits. There are the day-to-day crises, like the time the frozen water pipe burst and my daughter called me at work to say, "Mom, the sofa is floating and boy, are you gonna be mad when you get home!" (I was.) You may have a big crisis. Infertility, a failed business, a parent with Alzheimer's disease, or the death of a child. Our unity sustains us in our hour of need, when we wonder how we will get through the day, or how, once fractured, we could ever feel whole again. We must support each other's spiritual growth.

2. We must genuinely want our mate to be happy, while at the same time, understand that we are each responsible for our own happiness.

The first step is to play. Boredom is the great enemy of marriage. I am always impressed with my audiences' ingenious ways to have marital fun. One couple told me how they would drive to the local bar separately and pretend they did not know each other. The husband would "pick up" his wife, using his best lines. ("Hey good-looking, I haven't ever seen you in here before.") They flirted and laughed and both loved it.

Julia Simpson, of Discover Cards, told me how she and her fiancé had fun and still saved money for the Big Day. One weekend they turned her apartment into a miniature golf course and spent their Saturday night not with an expensive night on the town, but with a hilarious evening of putting through the house. It was silly and ridiculous and they loved laughing together.

George Bernard Shaw said, "We don't stop playing because we grow old. We grow old because we stop playing." Marriages grow old and tiresome without play.

How could you inject some more fun into your marriage?

The second step is to fight. You can't start your disagreements with, "And in this corner, in the blue trunks . . ." Still, avoiding arguments is not the goal. You need to stand your ground and put up a "good" fight. After all, who wants to be married to a doormat?

Fighting is tricky. You have to know that the squabble won't mean "It's over." Remember the much-photographed lover's quarrel the late John Kennedy Jr. and Carolyn Bessette Kennedy had in Central Park? Howard Markman, director of the Center for Marital and Family Studies at the University of Denver, says such lovers' spats are of great value. Fair and effective arguing can prevent the wounds that often fester and cripple a relationship. In his study of more than 150 couples, the good fighters took turns expressing their view, allowed each other to call "time-out" as necessary, and instead of attacking each other, waited until they understood their partner's position before they suggested a solution.

I guess that means I need to drop "And so's your mother!" from my fighting repertoire.

Do you and your spouse have a safe zone in which to disagree? Are your lovers' spats a chance to clear the air and start anew or are they saved like stamps until the next round?

Another factor in staying happy in marriage? Sex. Everybody knows that "sex sells." It "sells" in a relationship, too. David Meyer found in his study of married couples that "virtually every couple that had sex more than it argued were happily married." We can let our sex lives get stale and predictable or we can recognize the bond created by a healthy sex life and make plans to make it exciting. (This will probably not happen with the *TV Guide* in your hand.)

What is your sex-to-argument ratio?

3. You must be each other's world but you may not ask to be each other's universe.

The world "out there" can be a jungle. We need someone to comfort and encourage us, to believe in us, in sickness and in health. For a friend's bridal shower, I asked the invited guests to write the couple a letter offering their best advice for making romance and love last in marriage. One of the best came from happily married Rob and Shelly Humbach, who wrote simply, "Be each other's greatest fan."

## Free to Be Me

As much as a happy marriage requires a comfortable togetherness it certainly benefits from a healthy separateness. Rodney Dangerfield said, "We sleep in separate rooms, we have dinner apart, we take separate vacations—we're doing everything we can to keep our marriage together." We might not have to go that far; still, some of the most happily married couples I know are surprisingly both dependent and independent. They create a unique form of interdependence: they see themselves as very much a couple, yet definitely not joined at the hip.

My husband and I belong to separate health clubs. While rumors flew that twin beds were probably on the horizon, our marriage improved. He enjoyed lifting weights with the boys and doing his impersonation of Arnold Schwarzenegger. I liked the fact that no one at my club knew me as Joe's wife or the mother of three. I was just Mary. We also saw how blessed we were to have one another. The setup was good for both our marriage and our self-esteem.

Does your spouse know you are rooting for them? Are you the safe haven from the storms of life? Do you give each other the time you each need to be an individual?

## For Better or Worse? How *Much* Worse?

The list of flaws grows longer each year. Love handles appear on the midsection and your underwear could double as a dust rag. Six out of seven nights someone has bad breath, is overdrawn at the bank, or leaves the lid up. You know all his jokes. You can finish her sentences. You also know that you will always be there for each other because you have been there before.

André Maurois said, "Marriage is an edifice that must be rebuilt every day." Recommit to the construction process. Save a little of your best self every day for your partner. Put your best foot forward. Plan for romance. Because being married can be a wonderful thing.

## THE NEW SOLUTION:
## MARRIAGE AND ROMANCE

*When we can't keep up, we have a choice. We can:*

| DISCONNECT | CONNECT |
|---|---|
| **Forget romance**<br>I'm so tired—that's the last thing on my mind. | **Find time for romance**<br>"Let's give each other a quick back rub so we're not so tired." |
| **Focus on "to do" lists**<br>I'm hopelessly behind—I'll never catch up. | **Focus on each other**<br>"Tell me one good thing that happened to you today." |
| **Give up**<br>We've grown so far apart. This will never work. | **Give it a try**<br>I won't know unless I try. "Hon, want to go for a walk tonight?" |

When I got married twenty years ago, one of the readings at our wedding went something like this:

> There will be times in your marriage when you are so loving, you will think it impossible to ever have unkind words.
>
> There will also be times when you are so angry with each other you will wonder how you could ever have loved each other at all.
>
> This does not necessarily signal trouble in your marriage. It simply means that the feelings of love wax and wane. That is the nature of love. It is the commitment that you have made to your marriage that will keep your love alive.

The advice has proven true over the years. The love has waxed and waned. The best remedy was always finding ways to keep alive the cycle of connecting, disconnecting, and reconnecting.*

## MICROACTIONS

1. Simply decide to include a little more romance in your life. Say it out loud to someone. It doesn't require a partner. Treat yourself to a romantic movie alone and put the sense of romance back into your life.
2. Wipe the kitchen counters. (When my husband does this I consider it foreplay.)
3. Make love in another room, or better yet, go out of town.
4. Make a list of the qualities you admire in your spouse and mail it to him/her.
5. Brush her hair for her.
6. Surprise him with tickets to a sports event, theater, or movie.
7. E-mail a romantic message. Send one that says, "You were good last night!"

## IN REAL LIFE

Dear Mary,

When you mentioned that we were going to discuss being romantic, I thought, "Well, gee, I am really going to be lost in this part!" I am not in a serious romantic relationship right now but I do have a close male friend.

*(I highly recommend the reconnecting stage. Oh-la-la.)

After listening to the romantic ideas in class, I decided to let him know just how special he is to me.

My friend loves to listen to music and every morning on the way to work, he listens to his tape player. I decided to surprise him by recording my voice and telling him how much I treasure him and the time we spend with one another.

One early morning I called him and told him there was a tape in his work box that I thought he would enjoy. I had disguised my tape with the case of his favorite rock group. I told him I hoped he liked it and hung up. I was nervous for some reason and glad the call was over!

After work, he came over to my house with a stuffed animal. I was so happy! He sat me down and said he had never had someone make him feel as special as he had that morning. He said it made him cry. As long as I have known him never have I seen him shed a tear. Now I know how much we mean to one another. We ended the night with dinner and a movie. I will never forget that day.

Aloha and Mahalo Nui Loa,
Ronda M. Togashi
Honolulu, Hawaii

# CHAPTER 6

# Connecting with the New Kid on the Block

Before I got married I had six theories about bringing up children. Now I have six children and no theories.
—*John Wilmot, Earl of Rochester*

My seventeen-year-old daughter, Sarah, does her homework on the Net, takes a cellular phone on dates, and insists *everyone* gets a car for their sweet sixteen birthday. We had a fun discussion on whether or not it would be a "hot thing" to kiss a guy with a tongue ring. (We discovered a definite generation gap on this one.) My fourteen-year-old Emily wants $90 Harley Davidson boots, wears a fingernail polish color called "Trailer Trash," and is mad at me because I didn't save my bell-bottoms for her. This honor student absolutely cannot understand why I won't let her have a "very small, very tasteful" tattoo. Nicholas (ten going on nineteen) inquired one night, "Hey Mom, can two gay guys have a baby? How does a surrogate mom get pregnant?" (I wasn't horrified at the questions—only that we hadn't even gone over the regular birds and the bees yet.) And finally, with a look on his face that suggested he was about to ask about the Holy Grail, he whispered, "And really, Mom, you can tell me. I am old enough. Exactly what IS Victoria's Secret?"

We are not raising Wally and Theodore Cleaver. We are raising the new kids: entitled, worldly, high-tech—who because of the world they live in have been forced to grow up faster than most of us did.

According to a recent study we parents feel like underachievers. The research, conducted by a Washington group called Zero to Three, reported that as much as we love our children, we are exhausted and worry every day that we aren't spending enough time with our kids.

No offense intended, but . . . we needed a study to discover this? Just ask any parent. Ask them about the anguish of finding good day care, or the guilt over missing yet another school play or Little League game. Poll any parent at random and ask about single parenting, stepchildren, latchkey kids, too-little-too-late child support, and a host of other issues. You bet we are stressed.

The study also reported that 91 percent of new parents said they are happier than ever. I am not surprised by that finding, either. We adore our kids.

We are trying to raise different kids in a different world and our stress comes from being unsure if we are doing a good job. How much time is enough? Will our children be on the psychiatrist's couch if we don't make it back from the business trip in time for the father-son campout? Does a pierced belly button mean we have failed as parents?

Hey, don't expect me to know the answers to such tough questions! We're in the dark together here. No one has done it this way before. While I don't have any pat answers, I do believe what kids need is connection. They need to know who they belong to, that their family cares about each other— that they matter. We need to teach them how to live happy, successful, fulfilled lives.

We can do a good job, but we are probably not going to parent like our parents. Trying to do so only fills us with guilt. A woman spoke to me after my program and said, "I just feel so guilty about working while my two-year-old is at day care. Even though she seems happy and well adjusted, I actually compute the percentage of time I spend with her every day. It never seems like enough. My mother was always home."

One man said, "I'll be out of town for my daughter's dance recital, the culmination of a year's worth of lessons. I feel terrible." Another father complained, "I am divorced and had to move out of state to take a job. I feel so guilty for being so far away, but I have child support payments to make."

In a perfect world, there would be no out-of-town business, no missed dance recitals, and no divorce. Perfect it ain't. That doesn't mean we can't be wonderful parents and raise healthy, happy kids.

The first step is to set aside those Cleaver principles. The ones that say you will always be there, that you will never be too tired, that you will always be first and foremost interested in what your child needs at any given moment.

I fly home from a business trip at 10 P.M. exhausted, and before I put my suitcase down, I'm asked to help with the biology homework. I'd like to say I really care about the animal kingdom, phylum, genus, and species at 10 P.M., but I do not. I'd like to say I really care about my child's academic well-being but . . . well . . . sleep sounds really good.

I'll never forget coming home to Emily's plea, "I need a

model of the solar system . . . by tomorrow morning." Now, our house is pretty well stocked, but that week, we were fresh out of solar system models. Fortunately, it was December and I spied the Christmas ornament box. We constructed what I considered to be a dandy version of the nine planets, including our sun, using nothing but a coat hanger, yarn, and Christmas tree balls. It was an A project if ever I saw one. When the grade came home I was confused. A−. What on earth (sorry for the pun) could we have been marked off for? The grade sheet said, "Planet size not in proportion to actual planets." I wanted to march into that school and tell the teacher that if she could find two ornaments at Target that had the same diametric proportion as Pluto and Saturn I would . . . Oh, well, some things are better left unsaid.

The point here is, forgive yourself for being a human parent. Bionic you are not.

Second, instead of spotlighting all the things you aren't able to do and all the things you should do, think about how you can remain connected to your child by teaching them to live a good life.

I focus every day on the following nine areas. They won't make you a perfect parent and they won't guarantee you happy, healthy, tattooless children. They will give you a powerful way to stay connected to your family even if you are short on time and long on frazzled nerves.

## 1. Meet 'em where they are.

I've discovered I am more effective as a parent when I "meet 'em where they are." I can't make them be how I want them to be. I have to get on their level. I can't expect a three-year-old just being potty trained to lift the lid. (After all, I can't expect forty-five-year-olds to do it *all* the time.) It would be silly to think my teenagers are worried about how their room looks (very messy). They are worried about how *they* look. (Which means they will go to any lengths necessary to make sure they aren't messy.)

I was reminded of this lesson when I cashed in my frequent flyer miles last December, and Joe and I surprised ten-year-old Nicholas with a trip to Disney World. I told him he was getting out of school early to go to the dentist and instead took him to the airport. What a weekend we had! One of our favorite rides was the Pirates of the Caribbean in Fantasyland. As we disembarked from the pirate ship (into the gift shop, conveniently located on the way out when parents are in the "just buy it and let's get out of here" postride claustrophobic stage), Nick asked for a pirate gun. My first reaction was, "A gun? Hey, I am raising a pacifist. I donate money to gun-control causes. I refuse to own a firearm. I am *not* buying him a gun."

Seeing the look on his face, I reversed my opinion. "OK. All right. Let's pick out a pirate gun." I rationalized my decision. After all, this is the "Magic" Kingdom where all your dreams come true. What's one toy gun?

Next we went to Frontierland. We saw the magnificent Hall of Presidents program with fascinating details of the Civil War. We learned about our impressive presidents and what a fabulous country we live in. Nick fell in love with a Civil War pistol.

OK. We're talking *a really Magic Kingdom*, where your wildest imaginations come true. So what are two toy guns? We're on vacation.

By the time we got to the Extraterrestrial Alien ride (Tomorrowland) and he asked for yet another gun, it was clear we were on a mission to seek out faraway "lands," not in search of gold or riches or even some spices—no, we were combing Disney World for weapons.

Meet 'em where they are.

I could have ranted and raved. I could have denied him the artillery. I could have actually intervened when we went through "It's a Small, Small World" and he pretended to pick off the little twirling dolls with his Frontierland derringer. But I didn't.

I don't know if I am wrong. Initially, I had forbidden guns in the house. I gave up when, at age two, he chewed his toast into the shape of a gun and said, "Bang!"

I do know that when we got back to the hotel room Nicholas played with those guns for two hours, complete with elaborate diving shots to eliminate the evil guys, and sound effects that should have prompted nearby hotel guests to call the manager. I also know this is the kid who offers to help the English as a Second Language students with their assignments, who often mediates other children's conflicts, and whose fourth grade teacher describes him as "a great leader." I know he gently kisses his eighty-eight-year-old nana good-bye at the nursing home. He still asks me to cuddle and read to him. And he is also the little boy who kisses me good night and says (in an Arnold Schwarzenegger accent), "I'll be back!"

My friends Mary and Rolf Benirschke recently adopted two little Russian boys from an orphanage. Their sons, kids who have never seen guns, want to play with toy rifles! The concept apparently resides on the Y chromosome and I am helpless to change that.

Meet 'em where they are.

Emily and I had a talk one night about the homeless. It led to a serious discussion about the plight of these people, how they got there, and what their daily lives must be like. She then asked me, "What if you and Dad lost your jobs? What if we became homeless?"

I could almost see her wheels turning as she personalized this problem. I replied, "You are right, Emily. All of us could become homeless. What if you could take only one of your possessions to the homeless shelter? What would it be?"

I thought she would pick her favorite pair of blue jeans, her CD player, or her diary. Without hesitation she said, "My door. Teenagers need their privacy, you know."

Meet 'em where they are.

Emily told me how I could "meet her." It helped me to understand her recent changes in behavior and my reaction to it: like when I knock on her door to announce dinner, she steps out of her room, closes the door behind her, and says, "What?"

I feel annoyed. Like when she doesn't want me to attend her choir recital.

I feel hurt. Like when I ask about her day and she says, "I don't want to talk about it."

I feel rejected.

But when I learned that, if forced to pick only one possession, Emily would select what she values the most—her privacy—I stopped feeling annoyed, hurt, and rejected. And I can easily give her a gift of balance. I can meet her where she is.

What about you? How could you use the principle of "meet 'em where they are" to help connect with your kids? Are you letting them "act their age" or, because of stress and worry, are you asking them to be miniature adults?

2. Eat, drink, and be merry. Have dinner together as often as possible.

This advice may sound obvious because according to the Eat Dinner Together Survey conducted by Bruskin-Goldring

Research, almost three-quarters of us think eating dinner together is very or extremely important. Yet the study reported
that fewer than half (42 percent) of Americans eat dinner together every night. Sixty-six percent watch television or videos
during dinner.

Here's a thought. The families you are watching on TV are
not watching TV. Take the hint. TV-Free America and Niel-
sen Media Research (1997) report that during a typical week
children spend an average of 38.5 minutes in meaningful discussion with their parents and more than twenty-four hours
in front of the television. Throughout the year the average
child watches 20,000 commercials. All of a sudden I want my
children to be below average!

Remember, not everyone has dinner together *every* night.
Don't focus on the nights you aren't together. Make the nights
you are there special. You will find yourself looking for ways
to dine together.

How would you rate the quality of your family dinner time?
Could you raise it a notch by simply trying to do it more
often?

### 3. Be high-TECH (Touch, Encourage, Cuddle, Hug).

Talk about a fast, easy, effective strategy! With every action,
ask yourself if a touch could replace words. Instead of shouting
"It's time to get up!" stroke his hair, massage her back, or rub
their feet. Instead of yelling good-bye, give a kiss, and then
give them a smile. Instead of dictating orders, try a hug for a
job well done.

Years ago in my Psychology 101 course, I remember a famous experiment in which the researcher left a quarter in an
outdoor public telephone booth. She waited until someone
came along to use the phone and she watched to see the person

(as we all do) check the coin return. Then she would come running up and ask if the person had found her quarter in the return. If the researcher touched the person lightly on the shoulder the subject was much more likely to return the quarter than those who were simply asked! Touch is an underrated parenting technique.

It is never too late to be high-TECH. Ruth Ann Ferris of Aiea, Hawaii, wrote,

> My son took a Psychology/Sociology course this summer. On the last day of school he came home with his final grade. The grade was a B, so I am sure he expected at least one negative comment from me or his dad. Normally I would have said, "The B is good, but with a little more effort that B could have been an A. Instead, I gave him a hug and told him that I was proud of him for putting in the time and effort to earn a B. He waited to see if I was going to say anything else. When I didn't a smile came across his face and he said, "Thanks, Mom."

4. Worry less about being a wonder parent and more about being a fun-loving parent.

Sometimes we try too hard to be the perfect parent when loosening up would do the trick. I've stayed up until the wee hours of the morning getting everything just so for the birthday party, then I'd be bleary-eyed and cranky the next day from sleep deprivation. I now know my kids would rather do without hand-stenciled napkins that match the three-tiered dinosaur cake and instead would prefer I sit on the grass and watch the new boat float in the plastic pool.

If I could change one thing about the first seventeen years of parenting, I would have laughed more with the kids. I would have been less of a proper parent and more of a funny parent. When I messed up the most, it wasn't when I was gone. It was when I was there but I had no sense of humor. Laughter is the best connecter of all. You can laugh over the phone, via fax, on e-mail, in a card, at bedtime, in the car, while you are cleaning up—there is never a bad time to laugh and you don't have to be there in person.

Is there laughter in your house?

### 5. Pray with them. (Short prayers are best.)

Model spirituality in any way that aligns with your values. Kids are dying for (and literally because of the lack of) spiritual guidance. Church attendance is helpful but you need not limit yourself to organized religion. I remember seeing my father get down on his knees every night before going to bed and praying. No sermon could have had more impact on me.

Are you modeling your spirituality so your children can see it in action?

### 6. Use "guilt-free reading."

Read to your kids every day, even if it is only one line. We all have heard this advice, yet research suggests we don't read to our kids very much. An American Federation of Teachers survey found that only 52 percent of parents read to their children ages eight and younger on a regular basis. For children aged nine to fourteen, only 13 percent of us continue to read to our kids. These statistics intrigued me. If we know we should read to our kids, then why don't we?

First, it's because television, Sega, Super Nintendo, computer games, the World Wide Web, on-line buddies, chat rooms, movies, laser tag, and the telephone outdistance the time we spend reading.

Secondly, we have other expectations. Well, sure, we should read to the little kids, but older children? We reason that the school-age kids can read to themselves, so why do we have to? We have bigger fish to fry.

While diversions and expectations play a role, the biggest barrier to reading to children is exhaustion. Mine. When I have gone to work all day, I am exhausted by 8:30 that night. And when I stay home with the kids all day I am exhausted by 7:30! I really want to read to my kids but I'm *too tired.*

To solve this problem I developed what I call guilt-free reading. I select adult nonfiction books and I read only a page or two, and sometimes just a sentence. For example, one night I read one sentence out of *Life's Little Instruction Book* by H. Jackson Brown to my then ten-year-old. The advice read, "Have a dog." My daughter really wants a dog and I really do not want a dog. (I like dogs a lot . . . at other people's houses. We have a cat.)

What a wonderful discussion we had about getting a dog! What would you name the dog? What kind of a dog would you get? Are you going to get a dog when you grow up? Are you going to let your little girl have a dog? How do you take care of a dog? Why do you think I don't want a dog? We were on the bed talking for an hour and all I read were three words: "Have a dog."

I soon discovered there are countless fun, easy-to-read books that teach moral and life lessons and can be chunked down so even if I am totally bushed I can manage one tiny reading session. I want to recommend a couple of books to get you started.

*Live and Learn and Pass It On* by H. Jackson Brown features a collection of one-liners from people of all ages on what life has taught them. I read Nicholas a seven-year-old's advice from the book: "I learned that you can't hide a piece of broccoli in a glass of milk."

After a good laugh, this five-second reading led to a discussion: "Do you like broccoli? Cooked or raw? Why is it good for you? What former president hates broccoli?" We created an opportunity to laugh, learn, and feel close, and we only read fifteen words.

One father told me he e-mails his college son one sentence out of *A Father's Book of Wisdom* (also by H. Jackson Brown) every night. Whether he is coming home from the library or the pub, the son knows he can connect with his father before he goes to sleep.

*Storms of Perfection* by Andy Andrews. The author, a comedian by trade, wrote to hundreds of famous people from all walks of life and asked them this question: "What was your greatest rejection and how did you overcome it?" The one-page responses in letter form are fascinating, moving, and *short*. (Are you seeing a theme here?) We read one letter a night. I want to teach my children that sometimes life will reject you but you must resist the temptation to give up, and persevere if you really believe in what you are doing. Now if I *said* that to my kids they would respond, "Bla, bla, bla, yadda, yadda, yadda." But when I read them the letter from Amy Grant that explains how she suffered enormous rejection at the beginning of her career, that in one of her first public appearances, *no one* came—even her mother left and she was singing to an empty room—well, now they want to listen!

*Random Acts of Kindness* (The Editors of Conari Press), a book of one-page, heartwarming stories about people doing kind acts, is another wonderful example of guilt-free reading. We all complain about the violence in America, in our streets, schools, and workplaces. We place a bundle of criticism on the media for the graphic portrayal of violence in television and movies. I do not know how to solve the problem of violence in America. I do believe, however, if everyone were reading their child a daily kindness story, we could probably worry less about what the Hollywood producers were doing.

Every action should have more than one benefit, and guilt-free reading has so many benefits. It is a quick, easy way for me to teach moral lessons. I want to teach my kids the meaning of life but sometimes I fear I spend most of my time ordering them around: "Get in the car. Don't get out of the car. Please sit still. Move faster. Don't do that. Why didn't you do that? I don't care if you don't like it; that's what we're having for dinner!" These little books direct us to discuss the important issues in life. In addition, guilt-free reading increases their vocabulary. After reading *Storms of Perfection*, my daughter exclaimed, "For crying out loud! What does *adversity* mean?" Study after study shows that people with a higher vocabulary have a higher IQ, a higher income, higher self-esteem, and better health and longevity.

Another very important benefit is—*I* enjoy the books. They are adult books I wanted to read anyway. It models to my kids that I love to read. We all go to bed with good messages and positive thoughts. It gives us an easy way to emotionally connect. One evening my teenager had a nightmare. She woke me up with a book in her hand and said, "I'm scared. Will you read to me?" She had a built-in way to reach out.

The Guilt-Free Reading Program is also *flexible*. On those nights that *The Cat in the Hat* feels like *War and Peace*, you can always manage one sentence, one letter, or one little story, and you send a message to your children that reading is so important, we do it every night. You stay guilt-free.

7. Teach civility and the "facts of life."

Before we can solve the problem of violence in America we need to start with old-fashioned respect. Our kids see their heroes spit at umpires and their favorite teams empty the benches in a brawl. They watch their political leaders fling mud and celebrities punch the paparazzi in their plea for privacy. And they learn to follow their parents' example as Mom or Dad flips off the rude motorist! Our children won't learn civility if we don't seize every opportunity to model it daily.

Hard as it is for us to admit, our kids need to learn the "new facts of life." If you thought the old facts of life were hard to teach, just try these new ones on for size!

My daughter Sarah came home from sixth grade crying. During class that day a boy had made several derogatory, extremely sexually explicit remarks to her. Sarah was visibly shaken by his taunting and reported it to the teacher. The teacher's solution was to scold the boy and then reassign Sarah to another desk in the classroom.

I called to schedule a parent-teacher conference. I had a lot of questions. I was hoping this was all a big misunderstanding. I thought at her age the toughest topic should be getting a C— in computer science or wearing too short a skirt to the sixth grade dance. Unfortunately the teacher confirmed Sarah's account. So I asked, "Why was Sarah moved?"

"Well, you know, she was bothering the boy," the teacher said, defending her action. "Yes, I am sure she was. Sixth grade girls often bother sixth grade boys. Furthermore, I am quite certain that many of my male colleagues find me bothersome from time to time. It is, however, against the law for them to sexually harass me."

The teacher's actions were well intended, but what was she teaching these children? Sarah learned that if she complains about sexual harassment, she'll be "moved." The boy learned that sexual harassment is no big deal. We are doing a great disservice to both of them. Will my adult Sarah believe that as a manager her solution to the problem in her division is solved by simply removing the woman from the situation? Will she learn it is a waste of time to report sexual harassment? Will the boy learn that if he is accused of such behavior, the woman will simply be transferred out of the department?

These are not the facts of our children's lives. I also have a son, and as the parent of three, I learned early on never to say never: "My child would never lie, my child would never steal, my child would never sexually harass." That is why I want both my daughters and son to learn the real facts about race, gender, age, religion, and ethnicity. We will teach them by example.

What example are you setting?

### 8. Sprinkle your conversations with four phrases.

"I love you."

"Sure you can."

"Let's try again."

"I know you know what to do."

Listen to your interactions. How many "sprinkles" do you hear?

### 9. Let them do it for themselves.

One of the greatest gifts we can give our children is the gift of self-sufficiency. When the time is right, let them make their own bed, sandwiches, and mistakes. They probably won't say thanks now, but maybe someday . . .

## THE NEW SOLUTION:
### KIDS

*When we can't keep up, we have a choice. We can:*

DISCONNECT

CONNECT

Pray we don't make a mistake
I'm a terrible parent. I missed the soccer game again.

Pray with our kids
"Let me tuck you in. I want to hear all about the game today before bedtime prayers."

Lock horns over trivia
"Get up and clean your room right now or you're grounded. How can you live in such a mess?"

Lock hearts by touching
"Good morning! How about a quick back rub to loosen up those muscles before you tackle your room?"

Be guilt-ridden
I never spend enough time with the kids.

Be guided by connection
"Who wants to set the table for dinner?"
"Who wants to pick the book for tonight's reading?"

I remember a woman remarking to me as I cradled my newborn baby, "She sure is little. It's amazing how fast they grow." At the time I thought, "Of course she's little—she's a baby! She won't grow that fast."

I was wrong. Some days I catch myself wondering if I am going to deliver a boy or a girl and she walks in the kitchen wearing her softball uniform, asking for $20, and renegotiating her curfew. Time in this case is of the essence. Don't waste a second of the precious time you do have with your children wallowing in guilt. Do the very best you can and let love take care of the rest.

## MICROACTIONS

1. Go to the bookstore or library and find a guilt-free reading selection.
2. Turn the TV off for a week or until one hour before bedtime each night.
3. Ask your family about how you could improve dinnertime.
4. Count how many times you touched your child today.
5. Pay attention to the opportunities to teach good manners. Your children are watching.
6. Sit on the floor and play.
7. Marvel at your child, the miracle of miracles. And give yourself some credit for a job well done.

## IN REAL LIFE

Dear Mary,

I heard you speak at the AORN seminar and fully enjoyed it. Some of your stories hit home.

One of the most important statements I came away with was the connection between family and friends. My daughter is away at college. She graduates in May and will be starting her own life, probably away from Houston. This will be a crisis in my life because we are very close. I especially liked your e-mail idea. I plan to e-mail her every day with some thought of wisdom. She loves reading, so I plan to send her some of your suggested books.

Thank you for sharing yourself with us.

Sincerely,

Janelle Kister RN, CCRN

Houston, Texas

# CHAPTER 7

# The Family that Grays Together Stays Together

**The Stanley Family**   Barbara and Jim Dale

"Gramma called to say you should call her. But even if you don't, she'll call you because she's not too busy for you even if you're too busy for her."

> All that I am, or hope to be,
> I owe to my angel mother.
> —*Abraham Lincoln*

I don't remember June Cleaver ever lamenting about how to tell her father he must move to a nursing home; or Ward agonizing about what to do when his mother began showing early signs of Alzheimer's; or either of them worrying about elderly parents who didn't eat right or manage their finances well anymore. I don't recall them bemoaning their feelings of helplessness because they lived thousands of miles away. There were no *Leave It to Beaver* episodes dealing with a parent's loneliness after one of them dies.

Yet many of us will face—or are already facing—these painful issues. I don't have any pat answers for the sandwich generation, when many of us will be caring for children at the same time we are caring for aging parents. I will, however, tell you one thing: We better get good at it—fast!

By the turn of the century, the geriatric population is going to skyrocket. If only we'd had the forethought to have at least six kids so we could rope one of them into taking care of us. We are going to need a generation of adults who were taught as children that being loving and kind to the elderly is the right thing to do.

## The Ties that Bind

When I was growing up, my father drove down to the farm to visit his mother every Thursday afternoon. I'll never forget the sight of the two of them, just sitting together in the parlor and talking, not reading the paper or watching television, just laughing and chatting for over an hour. She died in 1993 at age ninety-six, and in all those years, I don't think he missed many Thursdays.

Perhaps you are thinking that not all elders are like my saintly grandmother. Good point. You are right. Some are not so easy to be around. We can, however, connect with them. My mother had an old-maid aunt, Aunt Cecilia. Do you remember the Old Maid card game and how you hated to get the Old Maid card? That card is an actual picture of my great-aunt Cecilia. This woman, bless her heart and God rest her soul, could drive you to drink. Even as a child I knew that she was eccentric and harmlessly—but profoundly—neurotic. Nevertheless, my mother mowed her yard, painted her house, drove her to church, took her to the doctor, and listened to her whine ad nauseam. It was not until I was an adult that I realized that my parents had enrolled me in their class, Modeling Respect for the Elderly: 101. I suspect many of you were enrolled in a similar program.

I want to enroll my children in the class, too. But times have changed. I can't drive down to the farm or mow my parents' yard to show them my respect. I'm not alone in this challenge. Mike Krzyzewski, coach of the nationally ranked Duke University men's basketball team, took a leave of absence when he realized he was not living his life according to his values. This kind of departure is nearly unheard-of for a winning coach in his profession. A mitigating factor was a conversation he had with his mother: "My mom would call and say, 'Mike, I don't want to take too much of your time.' It kind of hit me. My mom is eighty-three. I want to give her all my time. She gave me all her time."

Most of us are like Coach K.: very busy, very focused on our day-to-day lives and feeling guilty about not giving our parents the attention they deserve.

What to do? Think connection. Instead of groaning and moaning about how hard it is to deal with our parents' problems, we can instead strive to honor our mother and father. They will appreciate it and, equally important, we owe it to ourselves. Losing our parents will be one of the greatest pains we will suffer. If we have a good relationship with them, we will dearly miss the close times and the love we shared. If we have a less than great relationship with them, we will mourn the fact that we have forever lost the opportunity to make amends. Now is the time to model respect for our elders.

## The Memory Jar
> "Memories—Love's best preservative."
> (Og Mandino)

One year, as Mother's Day approached, I asked myself, "What does my mother want for a gift? She doesn't need another knickknack. I don't know her style or size in clothes anymore, and I used up all my good gift ideas last year" (I gave her a fruitcake). I was stumped. So I asked myself, "What does she *really* want for Mother's Day?" Then it hit me. What she really wants is to know that what she did made a difference in my life. Many of our parents worked hard, sacrificed—some even gave up their dreams so we could have ours—and all they really want is some feedback that their efforts worked! So to say thanks, I made my mother a Memory Jar.

I bought a cut-glass jar with a lid. Then on little pieces of paper I wrote down memories:

I remember our talk the night before I got married.

I remember calling you from the hospital and telling you
your first grandchild had been born.

I remember when I was thirteen and you wouldn't let me
shave my legs.

I put one hundred memories in the jar and sent it to her
with this note:

Dear Mom,

I'm busy. I know I neglect you. But I want you to know
that what you did for me made me a happy and healthy
person. I love you and think of you every day. Please read
these memories and think of me.

She was supposed to take out one memory a day. Yeah, right!
What did she do? Yep. She read them all the first day. The
point is, she read them and read them and reread them.

### The Most Precious Gift I've Ever Received

According to my mail, the Memory Jar is one of my most
popular ideas. Jeannine Hansen, PR director at AT&T, told
me, "As soon as I heard your story about the Memory Jar you
made for your mother, I knew my mother needed to have one.
So I gathered my three siblings and their spouses together and
we wrote enough memories for every day of the year, plus ten
extra for her to read aloud at her birthday party.

"Reading her daily memory is the highlight of her day.
Some days she cries and some days she laughs, but every day
she is reminded how much we love and appreciate her. She
said her Memory Jar is without a doubt the most precious gift
she has ever received."

Jeannine went on to describe one flaw in the program. "Believe it or not, my mother refuses to go out of town without her daily memory. So whenever they travel, my father counts out one for each day they'll be gone (he puts them in a Baggie) and doles one out to her each day! My biggest fear is that she's going to demand a refill next year!"

### Dad Would Like One Too

Another client told me about the Memory Jar he made for his eighty-year-old father. He wrote, "It was the best gift I've ever given him. He truly enjoyed reading each memory even though not all the memories I shared were positive. Sometimes I was a rotten kid! My dad is fairly disciplined and reading each memory became part of his morning devotional. I generated around one hundred memories. The bad news is, when the memories ran out, he wanted more, so now I have the challenge of digging back into our past together and finding more." The Memory Jar is an easy bridge for many fathers and sons who may be uncomfortable verbally expressing their love and admiration.

I made my father a Memory Jar upon his retirement after forty-eight years in the banking business. I contacted one hundred of my father's business associates, former employees, family, friends, and colleagues, encouraging them to relive a special moment they had shared. The most amazing thing happened. The little cards poured in and after nearly fifty years of hard work, "important deals," and financial success, not one person wrote about anything "big"!

They wrote about "the time you drove the four of us to St. Louis to take Ken Aspelmeier to the Army and you took the wrong turn. We had to drive twenty-five miles out of our way to get back. And on the return trip you took the same wrong turn, hence another twenty-five-mile detour. The first time

Herb thought it was funny. The second time—his comments are not repeatable." Or "I remember when we were twenty-one years old and we thought we were great baseball players. We played against the inmates at the Ft. Madison prison one day, and boy were we taught a lesson!" My favorite came from a former employee who wrote, "I remember during an ice storm, you called me and said, 'I know you live way out in the country. This job is not worth your life. Stay home, be safe, and I won't dock you any pay.'"

Not one person wrote about money or status or power. Everyone related a simple moment in time when they felt valued and connected to my father. I learned a priceless lesson. Perhaps my ambitious yearning to succeed, to get to the top, to make something of myself will mean far less in the end. Perhaps we all need to concentrate more on our connections with people—because that is what we will remember.

Peggy Nideffer of Bend, Oregon, had the same experience.

> I made my parents a Memory Jar. I was filled with such emotion when writing out the memories I thought I'd have to ice my eyes before going to work! My mom called in tears saying it was the most precious gift she had ever received and said my dad watches TV with his jar in his lap! You know, Mary, *not one* of my "precious memories" was of anything material. They were values, love, support, encouragement—all things from the heart. We all so desperately want to make a difference. I think I understand my mother's tears.

I receive hundreds of letters about the Memory Jar from all over the world. One of my favorites came from Jane Flowers, a perioperative nurse from Cambridge, Maryland:

Dear Mary,

My parents' forty-eighth anniversary was this past November. Like always, I had no clue as to what to get them for a gift. Then I remembered your Memory Jar.

My parents loved it. Amazingly, it was not until later that I learned just how much my dad liked the project. He writes a local column in our newspaper. He wrote an article on the Jar and its meaning. I don't think there is anyone in Dorchester County, Md., that has not heard of this project.

I've enclosed the article for you.

*My wife, Frances, and I were married 48 years ago. Our three children, Ann, Jane, and Dean, wanted to do something very special. Together, they came up with a gift that has brought not only them, but us, much joy. They brought us a "Memory Jar."*

*Taking a glass jar they filled it with over 300 of their memories of growing up in our home, the happy times, the sad times, the embarrassing moments. We have been instructed that each of us can take out a memory each day, read it, and recall that precious moment.*

*You can't believe the howls of laughter that erupted when Frances picked up the following memory to read: "Mom, do you remember when Dean let you use his Penguin sailboat? You stood up in the boat as it neared the wharf. A gust of wind hit you and you fell off the sailboat but you never got your hair wet. Dean's sailboat headed down the river. Dad was laughing so hard that even though he had the camera in his hands he forgot to take the picture."*

*Probably the most unforgettable moment was relived when I selected a memory that has been brought up at every birthday party for the last 30 years: "Remember Jane's fifth birthday and Mom forgot the candles for her cake? Jane was so upset that she cried as she mumbled, 'Everyone in the family had a cake with candles.' " Momma told Jane she was so sorry but then Momma had an idea. With the room dark, she came in with Jane's birthday cake and five Fourth of July sparklers a-spitting and a-sputtering. Jane's eyes almost popped out of her head.*

*There were some tears when one of the memories recalled, "Remember when Dr. Ken Burgwin came to our house and put Dufus (our 17-year-old Collie) to sleep—how we held him in our arms until he was gone and Dad buried him in the flower garden? How do you say goodbye to someone who has loved us beyond words? It is not an easy thing to do."*

*Our Memory Jar sits on the coffee table just waiting for tomorrow when Fran and I will select two more memories. What a fantastic idea to bring a family much joy, and as Jane says, "It was the cheapest we ever got off for your anniversary."*
*Dr. Thomas Flowers*
*Retired Educator, Author, Local Historian and Storyteller/ Folklorist*
The Daily Times *(Salisbury, Md.)*

Time and again people have described their parents' reaction with exactly the same words: "This is the most precious gift I have ever received." The scientist in me wants to know why this idea has been such an overwhelming success for my audiences and their families. I believe it is because memories are an anchor. In this turbulent, scary, and uncertain world in which we live, we often cope by disconnecting. Memories anchor us, they remind us that we *are* connected, and that makes us feel good.

> Memories anchor us to the past,
> strengthen us in the present,
> and preserve our love for the future.

### Making a Good Idea Better

The Memory Jar idea has many other applications. Why not help a new bride and groom bond by giving a memory card to each wedding guest so the new couple can share bits and pieces of their lives with one another? Use it as an anniversary tribute, a present to a teacher from the students, a fiftieth-birthday surprise, or an unforgettable high school graduation gift.

### A Magical Moment

I had the honor of speaking at the National Convention of the Perianesthesia Nurses. A few months later I spoke at their state convention in Florida. During my formal presentation, right when I got to the part about the Memory Jar, a woman in the front row raised her hand. My first thought was, "Not now, lady. Please! This is the middle of my keynote address!" But she kept her hand up and seemed sincere, so I called on her.

She stood up. "I heard your speech at our national convention and was on the committee that hired you. Also on that committee was a dear colleague who had breast cancer. After hearing you, our group collaborated to make her a Memory Jar. Our friend loved it, and we immensely enjoyed reminiscing with her. What an evening we shared! Shortly thereafter, she died. I had the opportunity to talk to her family just before coming to this conference and they thanked me profusely for the gift and said reading the memories has helped them immeasurably in their grief."

When she sat down I thought, "It's not nice to make the speaker cry in the middle of her presentation." A big thank-you to Nancy Saufl for reminding everyone in that room of the power and potential the Memory Jar has for connecting us.

## Your Family's Greatest Gift

As I explored ways to model respect for the elderly, a friend asked me, "What is the greatest gift a family can give itself?" The question haunted me for weeks. What in the world could it be? I wanted the answer, for whatever it was, I wanted to make sure my family had it. My obvious answer was love. But not all families love each other, I reasoned. So if love wasn't the answer, what was it? Why is it true that whoever you are, and whether you love them or not, you need a family? Psychologists would tell us the family fills our most basic need: to belong—to feel a connection to others. And that, I believe, is the greatest gift a family can give itself—a sense of belonging, a sense of knowing who we are and how we fit into the world by knowing who our family is.

## Lights, Camera, Action!

In 1993 I decided to find out more about my husband's family by interviewing my eighty-four-year-old mother-in-law, Esther. About a week prior to our appointment, I asked her to review a list of questions that I had printed in big bold type. On the scheduled day I brought along a videographer to videotape our conversation. (My VCR blinks 12:00 continuously so I needed professional help. You could use a home camcorder.) Then, for over an hour, I interviewed her, Barbara Walters style, in a review of her life:

"Esther, what is your earliest recollection? What were you like as a child? Tell me about your first kiss. Tell me about your wedding day. What was your proudest moment? What was your greatest disappointment? If you had your life to live over, what one thing would you do differently?"

She was brilliant! She shared story after story. She told about her life during the Depression when, as a young student nurse, she cared for children with contagious diseases like polio, diphtheria, and scarlet fever. She described how many of her colleagues, fifteen and sixteen years old, children themselves, often caught the diseases from their patients and died. She also related, with a twinkle in her eye, how she danced to the Lawrence Welk band in a ballroom in Chicago. Best of all, she smilingly recalled when a surgeon colleague invited her to his twelve-year-old daughter's dance recital. She delivered the punch line like a pro—the daughter grew up to be Nancy Reagan!

I had not heard any of these stories. On the other hand, I had never asked her.

## The Blessings and the Benefits

This videotaped interview is a great example of the life-balance guiding principle: every action should have more than one benefit. First of all, it brought Esther and me closer. You see, mothers-in-law and daughters-in-law have a natural rivalry. After all, we love the same man. My interest in her stories let her know how much I love and respect her.

After the interview, the list of benefits grew. I gave copies of the videotape to my husband and his brother as a surprise Christmas gift. It has become one of their most cherished possessions. It delighted my children as well. It not only helped them know their Nana better, it modeled to my children that old people are a library and all we have to do is ask the questions to hear great wisdom and insight. The tape continued to benefit Esther and me. I wish you could have seen her face on Christmas morning when she watched that video for the first time. Talk about connection! And when my husband, with tears in his eyes said, "Thank you," my Christmas was complete.

One fun benefit came the evening after the filming when Esther went to the community dining room of her retirement village for dinner. No matter how old or mature we get, we may still be tempted to indulge in a little game of one-upsmanship. Imagine the white-haired lady sitting next to Esther saying, "We didn't see you all afternoon. What did you do today?" And Esther nonchalantly replying, "Oh, not much. My daughter-in-law just interviewed me about my life and videotaped the conversation so generations to come will know me."

You are not going to top that one—no matter how many times you won at bingo!

## It Gets Better with Age

Connie Asher flew home to South Dakota to interview her parents. Although she feared it was going to be equivalent to parting the Red Sea, she said she was amazed at all the benefits.

> Dear Mary,
>
> I videotaped my parents two weeks ago. My dad is eighty-one and my mother is seventy-eight. It wasn't easy to prepare for. Dad was extremely nervous and I almost said, "OK, you don't have to do this." But we went ahead,

I hired a videographer, and I videotaped each of my parents.

Mary—these interviews made my trip home to see my parents one of the most memorable trips I've made in ten years! We talked more, we laughed a lot together, and I learned so much from them—I thought that I'd heard everything already, but I'll bet 50 percent of the stories they told were new to me. What a wonderful experience!

During the five days I was there I know Dad watched the tape several times. In other words, my parents really enjoyed it too. And the whole experience was such a great catalyst for conversation and family history.

Thanks so much for this idea, the questions, and for this gift that I now have for my kids and their children to come.

Warmly,
Connie

One year later I received this letter from Connie:

Dear Mary,

My father died last Sunday and I just got back from spending the week with my family. Thank you again for providing me with the information and the impetus to tape him last summer. The tape is so precious to us—as are the hours I got to spend with my dad through all the conversations about his life. What a gift!

Thanks again,
Connie

## "But Will These Ideas Work in My Family? We're, You Know, Kinda Different . . ."

Fortunately, these ideas work even if your family is less like the Cleavers and more like the Simpsons. I believe that you too will be amazed at the benefits you'll receive, even if you wouldn't exactly call your family "close." Many people have written to say how the Memory Jar and the videotaped interview have bonded previously estranged families. Others reported how it gave their widowed mother reasons to reach out and interact with the family, and how the reminiscing enriched their children's lives. My favorite stories come from families who are thrilled because these strategies gave them an opportunity to say what was really in their hearts. And it seems to work for just about every kind of personality. Sherron Kurtz wrote about her father and his reaction to receiving a Memory Jar: "This stoic man, who has never shown much emotion or expressed his feelings well, sat there and cried. We all did! It was wonderful. Dad says he is really enjoying his memories."

### Don't Wait

When your parents have passed on, these captured memories will be everlasting. My friends who have already lost their parents say, "Do you know what I would give to see my parents laughing, to hear their voices, to know how they really felt about life? Can you even begin to comprehend how much I'd love to tell them all the things I remember?" I received a call from Indy Blaney, who said, "Thanks for the idea to tape my mother. She has since died of cancer. My father and I recently watched the tape. You know, Mary, we heard her laughing. I'd forgotten it. There wasn't a lot of laughter in the last six months of her life. The laughter alone is worth everything."

## Do It for Today

I want to stress how many benefits there are for your family while everyone is still together. Jim Estey, sales director for Lucent Technologies, said the Memory Jar and videotaped interview prompted many phone calls and letters among him and his twelve siblings. He said he felt special joy knowing he was the one who initiated the projects and how long-lasting the benefits are. "Most of all," he wrote, "my parents have let us know how they get an emotional lift from the memories."

## Prune Juice Is an Acquired Taste

Cherishing your elders won't always be easy. Perhaps your parents let you down in some way. Maybe you frankly don't even like your parents. Or it could be your family has its own version of Aunt Cecilia. Regardless of your situation, I believe connecting with your elders, in whatever way is appropriate for you, will help to balance your life. I will never forget the woman who told me at a seminar, "You don't have to love your elders to care for them." And I would add, "You don't have to love your elders to connect with them either."

What about you? How could you use these ideas so your family can gray together and stay together?

I've made it easy. My book *Touching Tomorrow* contains everything you need to conduct a recorded interview with your elders. To order this book or for more information on the Memory Jar and Card Kit (a customized glass jar and thirty "I Remember" cards) please see page 237.

## THE NEW SOLUTION:
## OUR MOTHERS AND FATHERS

*When we can't keep up, we have a choice. We can:*

| DISCONNECT | CONNECT |
|---|---|
| **Groan and moan** | **Grow and model** |
| My last child has finished college. Instead of freedom, I am now burdened with my father who just had a stroke. The nursing home costs $140 a day! | This is a lot to handle. Of course I am going to feel overwhelmed. Who can help me? How can I show my kids the importance of loving the elderly? |
| **Resent my parents** | **Remember my parents** |
| My mother keeps harping that I don't call often enough. Can't she see how busy I am? | I am busy. I will make her a Memory Jar and remind her of my love. |
| **Reject my elders** | **Respect my elders** |
| My father tells the same stories over and over. It drives me crazy. | I'll just listen. Relieving these memories reaffirms that his life had meaning. Maybe I could tape his stories. |

"How far you go in life depends on your being tender with the young, compassionate with the aged, sympathetic with the striving, and tolerant of the weak and the strong," noted George Washington Carver, "because someday in life you will have been all of these." If we are lucky, when we are aged, we will be cared for by a generation of adults who understands our need to belong and who will take the time to show us that we are loved and appreciated.

Someone needs to show them the way.

## MICROACTIONS

1. Call your mother or father or grandparents for no particular reason at all. (This means even when you don't want anything.)
2. Ask your mother about the day of your birth.
3. Ask your father how he would describe a perfect day. (My father answered, "A little romance and a good round of golf!")
4. Call an elderly person and offer to take them for a ride.
5. Give long-distance phone certificates to your parents and ask them to call you.
6. Visualize yourself at age eighty-five. How do you feel? Where do you live? Who lives with you? What do you need?
7. Discuss the following poem with someone you love. This poem was written by a ninety-year-old woman in a convalescent hospital, and found in her room after she died. I have searched thoroughly but unsuccessfully for the author's name. I would have loved to have known her. If you knew the author, please contact me at the number given on page 235.

### A Crabbit Old Woman

What do you see people, what do you see?
Are you thinking when you are looking at me
A crabbit old woman, not very wise
Uncertain of habit, with far away eyes,
When you say in a loud voice—"I do wish you'd try."
Who seems not to notice the things that you do,
And is forever losing a stocking or shoe.
Who unresisting or not, lets you do as you will,

While bathing and feeding, the long day to fill.
Is that what you are thinking, is that what you see?
Then open your eyes, folks, you're not looking at me.
I'll tell you who I am as I sit here so still,
As I move at your bidding, as I eat at your will.
I'm a small child of ten with a father and mother,
Brothers and sisters who love one another,
A young girl of sixteen with wings on her feet,
Dreaming that soon now a lover she'll meet.
A bride soon at twenty—my heart gives a leap,
Remembering the vows that I promised to keep.
At twenty five I have young of my own,
Who need me to build a secure happy home.
A woman of thirty, my young now grow fast
Bound to each other with ties that should last.
At forty, my young sons are grown and are gone,
But my man is beside me to see that I don't mourn.
At fifty once more babies play around my knee,
Again we know children, my loved one and me.
Dark days are upon me, my husband is dead,
And I look to the future, I shudder with dread.
For my young are now rearing young of their own,
And I think of the years and the love I have known.
I'm an old woman and nature is cruel.
"Tis her jest to make old age look like a fool."
The body it crumbles, grace and vigor depart.
There is now a stone where I once had a heart.
But inside this old carcass a young girl still dwells,
And now and again my battered heart swells,
I remember the joys, I remember the pain,
And I'm loving and living life over again.
I think of the years all too few—gone too fast,

And accept the stark fact that nothing can last.
So open your eyes, people, open and see
Not a crabbit old woman, look closer—see *me!*

—Author Unknown

## IN REAL LIFE

Dear Mary,

Your idea made a big, big difference in my mother's life. When I attended your talk in January '96, Mom had just been diagnosed with advanced cancer a few months before. The Memory Jar was mailed to her with memories that ranged from the trivial ("I remember wrapping myself up in aluminum foil to make a spaceman Halloween costume, that lasted all of about three houses before it tore") to the amusing ("I remember the taxicab driver in Singapore who thought we were sisters"), to the insights into her parenting style ("I remember you were polite about my color by numbers pictures and enthusiastic about anything I drew myself").

Every few days, she'd phone in amazement to say some variation on "I can't believe you remembered *that.*" I found myself looking forward to those calls, and calling her if I hadn't heard from her for a few days. We'd always had a comfortable relationship, but it seemed to be improving. Clearly the memories were good conversation-starters. The day she read the one about "I remember you teaching us by example to always keep our promises," the floodgates opened. We talked about everything for almost three hours. Hopes. Fears. Wealth. Politics. Feminism. She told me she was proud of the person I had grown up to be. What she thought when my brother died. A good friend's ugly divorce and his daughter's reaction to his declaration of homosexuality. Who she thinks God is, and what doesn't scare her about dying.

Now hundreds of dollars in long-distance phone calls later, we've evolved a ritual 6 A.M. call every morning. We still talk about "everything." Some days it's just a quick, "Hi how's your weather?" We've talked about life and what is really important.

After the Memory Jar ran out and the you-knew-it-was-coming requested refills ran out, we tried something else. I had read Colin Powell's book and was intrigued by his list of rules at the end of the book, a one-page summary of his life philosophy. I asked my mom if she would like to work on her own "Lillian's Laws for Living." I've enclosed the result for you.

The story has a satisfying ending, too. When she was diagnosed with cancer almost two years ago, the doctors gave her six weeks to live. She's still around, still going to concerts, seeing friends, traveling a little. I am absolutely convinced that all the positive energy sent in her direction has a lot to do with her continued survival. I can never pay you back for what you gave me that night. I can only hope to pass it on.

Jaye Lunsford
Erie, Colorado

### LILLIAN'S LAWS FOR LIVING LIFE
#### by Lillian Lindner

*You can be anything you want to be, if you're willing to work hard enough.* No one else has the right to define you, your hopes, dreams, priorities, and goals. Never accept limitations or labels put on you by anyone.

*You control your environment.* You have the privilege and responsibility for making it what you want to live in—both your physical environment and the types of people you surround yourself with. If you abdicate that responsibility, you deserve to live in what you get.

*When you've really arrived, you don't have to shout about it.* Understatement is often the most elegant way to call attention to something (or yourself).

*Concentrate on getting an "A" for effort, and the rest will take care of itself.* Doing your best is more important than being the best.

*Keep your promises, no matter what.* If you're not certain you can keep it, don't make it!

*Always tell the truth.* Not only is it ethically correct, it's easier to remember than a lie.

*Moderation is always the wiser course.* There is no black or white, just shades of gray.

*Education is the most valuable thing you can acquire.* The truly wise person knows how much there is still to learn, and is willing to take lessons from everyone and everything in the world.

*All of your most valuable possessions are intangible.* Your skills, your friends, your health are more important than "stuff" you accumulate because it is useful, or beautiful, or amusing, or reminds you of someone special.

*Never let anyone pressure you for an immediate answer.* Any important decision is worth sleeping on. A good deal can stand scrutiny and will still look good in the morning.

*Make your own decisions, and take responsibility for the consequences.*

*Buck the trend.* Do what makes sense for you, no matter what "they" may think.

*Stand up for your rights.* No one else will do it for you.

*Keep things in perspective and pick your battles.* Identify what's really important, and fight as hard as you can for that; be ready to give in on anything else.

*Contemplating the nature of God is a procrastination technique—the world becomes a better place only through your positive action.* Even if you don't know what God is, you know what good works are. You should be out there making a difference!

*Tolerance is one of the most beautiful words in the English language.*

*Don't burn your bridges.* Keep as many options open as possible, as long as possible.

*Saying "thank you" is a great investment.* So inexpensive, and you never know when a kind word to someone else will give you a delightful payback.

# PART III

## *Connecting*
### with
# Others

# CHAPTER 8

# Rituals: They're Not Just for Breakfast Anymore

*I've never attempted anything so complicated as simplifying my life.*
—*Keith Gay*

I teach graduate classes for continuing education and often begin my lecture by asking the students to make a list of human beings with animal names: Larry Bird, Redd Foxx, John Deere, Catfish Hunter, Lynn Swan, and Ladybird Johnson. (The new one, of course, is Tiger Woods.) Initially the group groans, unable to think of any, but by the end of the session, we always come up with at least one hundred names. We often encounter a problem with this activity because our courses are four days long.

One time, in the middle of the second day, when I was talking about a totally different topic, a hand shot up. A woman in the audience asked, "Do you remember the lady from Mayberry, Aunt Bea? Don't you get it? It's a double, ant . . . bee."

I smiled. "Gee, what a clever idea. We're not talking about that now, but thanks for sharing." Thirty minutes later, another hand shot up. "Robin Leach. Don't you get it? It's a double, robin . . . leech."

At this point, it was very clear to me that no one was listening to a word I was saying. We had a new game going—Double Animal Names. I could see everyone's eyes glaze over as they began scanning for dual combinations.

The original purpose of the name exercise is to remind the students of the principle:

You get *what you focus on.*

You already have a lot of experience with this axiom. My guess is, you are probably pretty good at what you do for a living. How did you learn to excel at it? You *focused* on it. You found ways to repeatedly practice what you wanted to learn. This principle works in the life-balance arena as well. If you consistently focus on connection strategies that bring harmony into your life, harmony is exactly what you will get.

## Use What You Already Know

An easy, effective, and fun way to focus on connection is to use rituals. Meaningful rituals give our lives some predictability and stability, providing a sense of security and comfort. We already know how to use rituals. We have turkey on Thanksgiving, cake at birthdays, and pumpkins at Halloween. We have morning and nighttime rituals, and hello and good-bye rituals. By creating your own personal rites you can connect with those you love and have smoother sailing.

## Power Breakfasts

Kids seem to have a knack for stretching our inner resources. While all ages can cause a ruckus, the squabbles often come to a crescendo around puberty. Adolescents spend half their time truly wanting and needing the love, attention, and guidance of their parents. They spend the other half wishing their parents did not live on the same planet.

Dr. Anthony Wolf, author of *Get Out of My Life, But First Can You Drive Me and Cheryl to the Mall?*, explains that this conflicting and emancipating behavior is normal, necessary, and no cause for emergency psychiatric hospitalization (mine). But that does not make it easy to live with. So when my oldest daughter turned eleven, I used a humor ritual, attempting to bridge the ever-widening gap.

Every morning at 6:30 A.M., she and I would read the newspaper comics together. I'd have a cup of tea, she'd have hot chocolate. We'd point out the funniest ones ("Oh, Mom, read this one"), and watch the serial comics progress, trying to predict what would happen tomorrow. She'd cut some out for friends and teachers and sometimes we'd mail one to Dad at his office. While the rest of the clan slept, she and I enjoyed ten minutes together.

It was the only period of *guaranteed* civility we had each day and neither one of us would miss it. I was greeted each morning with, "Come on Mom. Let's read." Reading the comics became as important a morning ceremony for her as brushing her teeth. (No, not as important as brushing her hair—but important nevertheless!)

## Double the Pleasure—Double the Fun

Our early-morning rendezvous illustrates again that important guiding principle:

Every action should have more than one benefit.

Notice I did not say, "Do two things at once." After a while, stacking every task so you do two or more at a time will make you crazy. If we learn to concentrate on benefits instead of laundry lists we will realize just how much we are accomplishing.

Our comic sessions had many benefits that still linger today. Not only did Sarah and I enjoy laughing together, we had time alone together. We learned to share our thoughts and trust one another. I believe that if Sarah, now age seventeen, needs to confide in me . . . that she is getting an F in Spanish, or she doesn't want to go to college after all, or . . . if she wants information on birth control or other moral issues, she knows that I will always have time for her.

I am not so naive as to suggest that our children will always share their innermost concerns and fears with us. In fact, most of the time they probably won't. But if the opportunity is there . . . Perhaps, as parents or as the adult friends of adolescents, all we really have to offer is the opportunity to talk with us— no matter how old our "children" are.

## You're Never Too Old

A woman in one of my seminars shared her favorite ritual. She very excitedly explained how each Easter morning her husband would hide colored eggs for their two children and how much fun the whole family had watching the kids happily search for them. She said that even though her children had grown and moved away, her kids still called every Easter morning and asked, "Has Dad hidden the eggs yet?" Then they would dash over to their parents' home to begin the ritualistic hunt. She seemed to truly delight in relating this story so I asked her, "How old are your children now?"

She grinned. "Forty-nine and fifty years old!"

## Remember Your Blessings

I started our favorite family ritual when the kids were still in the high chair. Each night at dinner we ask each other, "What one good thing happened to you today." We all take a turn at sharing a bright moment. Not only does this set the tone for dinner (we have less time for whining and complaining), we also learn about things we wouldn't have heard without asking.

One night we heard, "The nice thing that happened to me today was the teacher did not holler at me." This statement prompted us to inquire, "What do you mean?" We learned about Sarah's classroom concerns, an easily remedied problem once we got the facts.

Another night Emily said, "The nicest thing today happened in social studies class. We're studying the Holocaust and a concentration camp survivor spoke to us. Do you know my generation is the last that will hear directly from those who actually experienced it?" With compassion and fervor she described her lesson. Our reaction? We were spellbound.

Imagine if I had simply asked, "How was school today?" I'd have heard, "OK." Our simple question guided us to a memorable and worthwhile discussion of important issues.

## Drawing Power

Peggy Beardsley of Minneapolis has a lovely Thanksgiving observance. Every year when three neighborhood families gather for dinner the hostess covers the dining room table with butcher paper and gives everyone a set of markers. Each guest then draws a place mat representing something for which they are thankful. She says the artwork connects every-one with themselves and with each other as they review their blessings. Peggy said the ritual originated with her friend, B.G. Hook, of Milwaukee. One year all the relatives showed up at B.G.'s house for Thanksgiving, and without enough linens to go around, she dreamed up this innovative solution.

## It's Never Too Late to Start

Dorothy Cullen, author of *Traits of a Healthy Family*, wrote, "To children, once is a tradition." She's right. I was reminded how easy it is by this letter:

> Dear Mary,
> Rituals can begin at any time. My children are twenty-nine and thirty-two years old. This year I decided that we would go out for dinner for our birthdays. My daughter's birthday was first and we had a lovely time visiting and being together. Neither of the children are married nor do they live at home, so our lives are fragmented.
> We went out to dinner on my birthday in August and for my son's in September. Each one was as enjoyable as the last. But on my husband's birthday, we were all going in different directions. I suggested we forgo going out for dinner on Dad's birthday. My daughter informed me, "Mom, we *always* go out on our birthdays!"
> A ritual has been established!
> Sincerely,
> Betty Davies
> Independence, Missouri

## The Ceremonial Crouton Ritual

The beauty of traditions is that they can take any simple form. Jan Kepler wrote,

> My husband, John, is a wonderful father to his twenty-three-year-old son and my stepson, Christian. Their relationship always touches me because my father was a mean and violent alcoholic. Since Christian was a little guy, John has always taken a crouton from his salad and put it on Christian's place mat at the beginning of dinner. Chris still loves getting the first crouton from his dad. It's a curious little ritual, but it brings back memories of sweet innocent times in our son's life.

The crouton ritual intrigued me. Why does this persist? What does it mean? Why would a twenty-three-year-old still want a crouton on his place mat? I wonder if it is because only John and Christian can share it. It joins them in its exclusivity. It reminds them that they belong to each other.

## Controlling Time with Rituals

Rituals are especially helpful in keeping us involved with those we really care about because they have nothing to do with time. Many of us feel we have little control over our schedules. This is particularly true for those in professional sports. Becky Baylor, wife of Don Baylor, the manager of the Colorado Rockies major league baseball team, told me there is a Rockies schedule by every phone in their house and their lives are dictated by it. Her good-bye ritual with Don is to always kiss him and say "I love you" before he leaves the house. Becky and Don cannot control the time they spend together, but they can control their feelings for each other, despite the frequent separations. They use a time-tested approach that works for them.

## Ham and Cheese on Rye

I spoke to the Wholesale Florists, and in researching their industry, discovered they have some unique work-life conflicts. By definition their days are long. The flower trucks arrive at 4 A.M. and the florists are still dealing with retailers at 7 P.M. In addition, they order flowers from all over the world daily, dealing with different time zones, languages, and money systems. I couldn't wait to hear how they used rituals to connect, given the often long separations from their loved ones.

A man offered this example: "My wife makes my lunch every morning and each day before she packs my sandwich, she takes a bite out of it." My first thought was, "Does the health department know?"

His wife was sitting next to him and I asked, "Why would a very nice woman like yourself do such a thing?"

She laughed. "The first time, to be honest, I was just hungry. My husband called me from work and said, 'Hey, what's this?' I said, 'I just wanted you to think about me.' "

Her husband chimed back in. "And I do. Every day, no matter how busy and chaotic the morning has been, at lunchtime I think of her."

"I know he's thinking of me. It connects us. So every day I take a nibble."

My audiences tell me they can't keep their lives in balance because they don't have enough time or money or they can't always be "there." Do you see how connection defies time and economics and distance?

Both Becky Baylor and the florists reminded me of an important principle:

> We cannot control time; we can control
> our connections.

## Rituals and Business

Jeff Baenen, vice president of sales and marketing for Du-Charme McMillen, must travel coast to coast and says he uses rituals to stay sane on the road. Frequent travelers know the road warrior's life is not as glamorous as it is cracked up to be. So Jeff uses rituals to conserve his energy. "I stay at the same hotels, rent the same car, and eat at the same restaurants. That way I'm not spending energy on mundane decisions. Not only can I then concentrate on my business, I can delegate some of the tasks since the decisions are already made."

Another woman said she uses rituals to help her business, too. She lamented one day to her husband that she was stressing out because she felt she was ignoring her clients, but she just didn't have enough hours in her day to call each of them. Her husband remarked, "Doesn't Mary say, 'When you can't keep up, connect?' "

"So I spent an hour writing a one-page newsletter with useful tips to let them know I was thinking of them. Presto! I was back in balance. That connection thing works in business, too!"

## Is It a Ritual or a Rut?

I have the opportunity to ride on many planes each year and my seatmate, upon learning my vocation, almost always whispers, "Do you do private consultations?"

"Well, no," I reply, "but we have a while before we land. What seems to be the trouble?"

After a long litany of concerns I ask, "When was the last

time you got rid of something?" My question often catches them by surprise. "Gee, I never considered that."

In mathematics, when you add and add and add without stopping it's called *infinity*. In life, when you add and add and add without stopping its called *insanity*. Something's gotta go.

Each year we take on more responsibilities at work, attempting to do "more with less." We commute farther. We carpool to soccer, care for our parents, borrow more money, and make bigger plans. About the only thing we don't do more of is sleep. *Then* we wonder why our lives seem unstable. Every once in a while we need to dispose of a few "things." So what can you delete?

## What Would Santa Think?

A good place to start are rituals that are no longer meaningful and useful. Holiday observances are often the biggest culprits. I read a statistic that said, on average, parents play with their children for "X" amount of time on Christmas. What do you suppose "X" is? Two hours? One hour? Thirty minutes?

The answer is seven minutes! I was outraged! Why, those inconsiderate, cold, heartless parents! Don't they care about their kids? How could they wrap all those gifts, put up the tree, make a wonderful dinner, and then play with their kids for only seven minutes? What is this world coming to?

Then I thought about what *I* do on Christmas Eve. I iron the tablecloth, set out the china, polish the silver, roast the turkey, mash the potatoes, make the relish trays, and then I shout at everyone: "Put on a clean shirt . . . take some of that makeup off . . . let Nana sit there . . . I know you don't like beets, but Grandma does . . . Let him play with your toy . . . What do you mean it's broken already. . . . If you ask me one more time when dinner will be ready! . . ."

And then when I have put everyone into a festive mood, we have dinner. What do I do next? I reverse the process. I get the Tupperware out, put the leftovers away, wash the mashed-potato pot, clean the silverware. . . . I realized I wasn't playing with my kids for more than seven minutes, if even that. Here was a tradition that had lost its meaning. Sure, having a feast was fun, but not the way we were going about it. So after a family meeting, we agreed the melee we called Christmas dinner had to go.

In its place we put in a new rule: *Christmas Eve supper cannot require cooking.* We get pounds of precooked shrimp or one of those delicious ready-to-eat hams, and serve Havarti cheese and French bread, fine wine, and complete the meal with some fabulous pastries from the bakery around the corner. When our feast is over, because there are no pots and pans or Tupperware to deal with, we initiated a new ritual. We turn out all the lights in the dining room, light twenty-five candles and the Christmas tree, and sing Christmas carols to candlelight. As a grand finale, eighty-eight-year-old Nana sings "Silent Night" in German, the way her father used to sing to her.

Here is Emily's first-grade interpretation of our new ritual.

"This year my family stayed home for Christmas. It was the first time in thirteen years we stayed home.

We usually go to my grandma's house in Iowa. My grandma and grandpa were going to come but my grandpa had a heart attack. But my uncles and aunts and nana came. We ate good food. Then we sang songs."

What are my children going to remember? That there were no lumps in the mashed potatoes? No wrinkles in the table-cloth? Or that every Christmas Eve we sang Christmas carols to candlelight?

Please understand—I am *not* insisting everyone stop cook-ing on holidays. This strategy worked at my house because (as I have confessed) I can't cook. The real reason our house has a kitchen is for the resale value. Still, I was secretly fantasizing the family would plead, "Oh pleeeease, Mom, it just wouldn't be Christmas without your delicious cooking!"

It didn't happen.

## It's a Big Club

You'd think I could have figured out how to simplify holidays a lot sooner than I did. But I've learned I am not alone in seeing the obvious. Connie Nikolaidis of Tucson, Arizona, wrote,

> I had just about decided this year that holidays were meant for other people; no matter how early I started or how organized I tried to be, I worked as an indentured servant in my home on the holiday and for several days prior to and after the holiday. The most distressing part was that I was my own boss. I had no one to blame but myself. Your advice to connect with myself and get rid of a holiday ritual was particularly helpful and relieving to hear. I can truly say in a world of mass confusion, disorganization, and utter chaos (my own), you seem like the Motel 6 logo, leaving the light on for me and the rest of the completely overwhelmed. I hope to pass this wisdom to my family and friends.

## In the Spirit of Compromise

Julie Wassom called to say my Christmas Eve story had inspired her to stop sending Christmas cards. She found the process expensive, time-consuming, and stressful. Yet, when she announced her plans to her husband, he said, "But I love giving and receiving cards. What if we take one afternoon in December, set up an assembly line for stamping and addressing, and the whole family will help?" Julie said the ritual is reborn and is now more meaningful than ever.

Another woman told me, "When I heard your Christmas Eve story, I realized there was one ritual I needed to eliminate. In Hawaii, *ohana* [family] is very important. So to honor my parents who live in San Francisco, I call them every Saturday at 8:30 A.M. Although I love the talks, I often resented the Saturday obligation. I couldn't go to the beach or begin my household chores, or make other plans. So with your inspiration, I called my parents and asked them if we could change the calling time from 8:30 A.M. to 4:30 P.M. To my surprise they said, 'Good idea!' You can't know how much changing this one little thing has balanced my life. I just got back from the beach with my friends and now I am really looking forward to talking to my parents this afternoon. I never thought changing one little ritual could make such a difference."

## What I Hear You Saying Is . . .

These examples demonstrate an important aspect of changing rituals. Check it out first! Listen carefully to what your family is *really* saying. Rebecca Mehaffy told me about her experience in abandoning a ritual. Each year on their birthdays, her children would come downstairs in the morning to find the kitchen decorated with brightly colored streamers and helium balloons, a birthday cake on the counter, and a beautifully wrapped gift. A few days before her daughter Jill's eighteenth birthday, Jill approached her mother. "I don't want to hurt your feelings, but I'd like to ask you to skip the birthday decorations. I am eighteen now and what I really want for my birthday is to be accepted as an adult. I need to put aside these childish celebrations. I am a woman and just a little too old for this sort of thing. I'd die of embarrassment if my friends found out my mother decorates the kitchen on my birthday."

When Jill came down to the kitchen on her birthday, Rebecca had granted her wish. Jill's face dropped. "Where are the balloons and streamers? Don't I get a cake? What about my present? Did you forget it's my birthday?"

Rebecca was confused. "Jill, what about 'I'm a woman now. I want to be accepted as an adult. I'm too old for such foolishness'? You said you didn't want me to decorate for your birthday."

Jill looked sheepish and exclaimed, "Well, you didn't *believe* me, did you!"

The streamers and balloons were up by the time Jill returned from school. The birthday rite, Rebecca said, is alive and well.

## The Tootsie Roll Ritual

The importance of rituals was brought home to me when I was just a little girl. My grandparents lived on a farm in Iowa and we visited often. I would fling open the front door of the farmhouse and then race as fast as my little legs would carry me, through the parlor, through the living room, through the kitchen and into the old pantry, where I would wait excitedly, because I knew what was coming next.

Tall and lanky Grandpa, always dressed in his striped farmer bib overalls, would slowly and silently stroll through the house as well, until finally, in what seemed like an eternity to a child, he'd come sauntering into the old pantry. He would reach up high on a shelf, take down the "magic box" of Tootsie Rolls, and with a big smile, stoop down to my level. I would reach in and grab as many Tootsie Rolls as my little fists could hold. This unconditional offering was symbolic while growing up in a house with five brothers. Everything seemed to have limits. Grandpa's Tootsie Rolls were the exception, and it created a special bond for us.

Years passed. I grew up and got married. When I became pregnant with my first child I wanted to find a special way to tell my father (Grandpa's son) that he would soon be a grandpa. So, instead of telling him I was pregnant, I just sent him a box of Tootsie Rolls. Upon their arrival, I was told that my dad, a kindhearted but reserved German man, sat down and cried.

He wasn't crying because I was going to have a baby. As he held the box of Tootsie Rolls, he remembered the relationship he'd had with his own beloved grandfather. He remembered his father, who'd been gone for years, and he understood that he had now assumed the revered role of Grandpa Schulte. He remembered how he had watched me run to his father to collect fistfuls of Tootsie Rolls, and he cried with the joy of knowing his little girl was now a grown woman having a baby of her own. Those emotions spanned five generations! *That* is the power of ritual.

What time-honored rituals can you create that will stand the test of time?

## THE NEW SOLUTION:
## RITUALS

*When we can't keep up, we have a choice. We can:*

### DISCONNECT

**Focus on problems**
"I work the day shift and you work the swing shift. It's hopeless."

**Use outdated, meaningless rituals**
"We will visit both sets of grandparents, all four sets of divorced parents, and your cousin on Hanukkah."

**Add until you are insane**
"I am so tired at night. But I have to put all the laundry away (or mow the lawn or wash the boat) first."

### CONNECT

**Focus on balance**
"I want to feel close to you. Let's brainstorm some ideas that will work for both of us."

**Use updated meaningful rituals**
"Let's think about how our family wants to celebrate without running everywhere."

**Delete until you are balanced**
"Each child can take clean clothes out of the basket during the week. I'm going to get some sleep so I can enjoy the concert tomorrow night. We can take turns with Dad's chores, too."

Whether it is the cup of coffee every morning while you work the crossword puzzle or the three practice strokes you always take before every putt, meaningful rituals keep us on an even keel. When your anxiety level rises and you feel your life is a few sandwiches short of a picnic, ask yourself, "What routines could I use and which ones could I reject that would connect me with my life?"

## MICROACTIONS

1. Most rituals are tied to a cultural universal, such as language, religion, economy, art, food, celebrations, music, touch, family units, etc. Make a list of your family's rituals. Are they tied to a cultural universal?
2. Circle your favorite ones.
3. Put a question mark by the ones that aren't so meaningful anymore.
4. Ask your family how they feel about them. Discuss whether anything should be added or eliminated.
5. Make a list of the rituals you had as a child. How did they make you feel?
6. Institute a morning routine that connects you to yourself or your God.
7. Develop a good-bye ritual that connects you to someone you love.

## IN REAL LIFE

Aloha, Mary:

Just had to write and say thank you for your many insights.

First, it was a joy spending time with you and seeing your family in action. *The Waltons are alive and well and living in the LoVerde home!* I was particularly impressed that you "practiced what you preached" with your family rituals. Whether it's "alone" time with each of your children every day, or the "What's one good thing that happened to you today?" question at the dinner table—these traditions personify your commitment to nurturing each other in the midst of a busy lifestyle.

Thought you might like to hear you motivated me to follow up and try several of your routines in our home. There could be no better testimony to their effectiveness than what our son said one night. We were about finished with our meal and Andrew asked hopefully, "Are we going to do that prayer thing tonight?" I'd always heard that if the only prayer we ever said was "Thank you," that would be enough. Obviously, that concept is understandable to a nine-year-old because Andrew already knew that expressing his gratitude was a prayer and he felt good about it.

You propose that "connection is the key to the quality of life." You make the point that most of us isolate ourselves when we get overwhelmed, and we should do just the opposite. Instead of withdrawing from our family and friends when things get crazy, we need to reach out to them. The secret in balance, as you say, is not working harder or smarter but making time for loved ones.

So true. That was certainly my insight from the *Tongue Fu!* media tour. I couldn't believe how many people warned me in advance, "You're going to get exhausted," "You'll be a walking zombie by the end of all that jet lag." Several people said, "You're going to be rushing from place to place, you won't have time to hook up with friends." Thanks to your advice, I did just the opposite. I went out of my way to connect with Hawaii neighbors who had moved to the mainland. I scheduled in time for National Speakers' Association buddies when I was in their city. As a result, the tour was the best of both worlds.

Because of your astute insight, I realized the celebrity moments (noshing strawberries in a presidential suite, national TV shows, getting picked up by a white stretch limo, etc.) would have all been essentially empty experiences if they hadn't been grounded and balanced with time spent with friends. Success is indeed sweetest when it is shared.

Mary, thank you for sharing your message with the world. You remind us in the midst of our hectic lives—that loving relationships (not fame or fortune) are the enduring reward of life. If we are too busy for friends and family, we're too busy! Your lesson has already positively influenced me, and will continue to shape the way I choose to spend my time in the future. Mahalo.

Sincerely,

Sam Horn

Author, *Tongue Fu!*

# CHAPTER 9

# Policies: There Is a Method to This Madness

*Method is like packing things in a box; a good packer will get in half again as much as a bad one.*
—*Richard Cecil*

My audiences tell me they are exhausted from trying to fill too many shoes. They are overbooked, overcommitted, and overwhelmed. We often get in this pickle because we do not know how to say no without risking our relationships or feeling guilty.

When our dance card is full, we can borrow a successful business practice and stay in control. Businesses say no with policies. They are not singling out any individual. They have thought long and hard about how to run their company and apply their policies across the board. There are return policies, investment policies, and insurance policies—in fact, most of what they do is influenced by a policy.

I saw this strategy in action when I attended a National Speakers Association convention a couple of years ago. The keynote speaker did a fabulous job and received a standing

ovation. After his program, about twelve speakers from our
state chapter gathered around him to offer congratulations. In
the magic of the emotional moment, we asked him if he would
come to speak at our chapter meeting that fall. I'm thinking
to myself, "The guy is going to have to say yes. We've just
shown him how much we care about him and how wonderful
we think he is. With all this peer pressure he's not going to be
able to get out of it." I almost felt sorry for him.

We have all been in similar situations. Unable to think of a
graceful escape, we say yes when we mean no. That's when the
trouble starts.

I was surprised by his reply. He said, "I would love to come
speak to your chapter. I have a policy that I do two NSA
programs a year. I'm doing this one and I'll also be presenting
at the national convention this summer. Perhaps we'd like to
look at next year."

What did he say to us? He said no, didn't he? But did it feel
like no? It did not.

The reason it didn't feel like a rejection is because he had a
*policy*. He wasn't spurning *us*. He had clearly thought out ahead
of time what he could and could not do. He had decided that
he wanted both to give service to others and have time for his
other important goals. He simply established a personal rule
about how many NSA programs he would offer each year.
The policy allows him to live his life "connected" and feel
good about his choices.

I came home so excited. Policies. What a great connection
strategy! I had always been told that when I felt stretched by
multiple demands I needed to understand my values and live
my life according to my convictions. I knew what was important to me; I just had a hard time telling other people
because I'd run the risk of alienating my friends and col-

leagues. This masterful speaker showed me how to balance and keep my relationships intact.

As luck would have it, I had lunch with my mentor, Roswitha Smale, a few weeks later. She told me she was writing a "personal policy book" for herself to help guide her in decision-making. The universe was hitting me over the head with this idea.

## Policies: A Short-Cut to Connection

I began researching. What exactly is a policy? Webster defines a policy as "wisdom in the management of affairs." I was on to something. I asked my audiences about their policies. Why do they work? Nelda Coats wrote to me, "The perspective of a policy is great because it removes the decision to a third party instead of making me the bad guy!" In my survey of several thousand people I discovered policies are centered mostly around family and faith. The boundaries help keep personal, family, or spiritual time sacred while limiting distractions.

Most respondents reported their policies helped to avoid major-league overwhelming guilt. Some of my favorites include:

- We do not discuss bad behavior or problems at dinner.
- We don't write checks on Sunday.
- The car doesn't move until everyone is buckled up.
- Half of all allowance money every week goes into savings.
- We always light a candle at dinner to add to our quiet talking and eating time.
- No one is allowed to say "shut up."
- I say no to any commitment that takes me away from my children in the summer.
- Thursday is Mom's night out.
- We always say grace, even in public.

- Nothing takes precedence over Sunday morning church.
- Schoolwork comes first.
- Extra money gets earned. As a single mom, I taught my boys there are no handouts.
- One day a week we do not get in the car.

Imagine, if we adopted those simple policies, how much more tranquility we would have in our daily lives.

## When You Are Running Low

One man confessed his weakness was running late in the morning so his policy was always to fill up the gas tank when the gauge reached the one-fourth mark, so that he'd never have to stop at a station on his way to work. Every woman in the room laughed. "Why?" they all asked. "You've got a whole quarter of a tank left!" This policy might interfere with the intimate conversations many couples share, when they get into the car and the man turns to his beloved and whispers, "So how long has the little gas light been on?"

My husband recently filled up my twelve-gallon tank. In a tone that suggested I should be alarmed he said, "It took 11.89 gallons!"

I smiled. "See, I told you it wasn't empty."

## Twice as Nice

Denise Hadley, an account manager in a high-stress job at Lucent Technologies, worked long hours, often missed dinner, and as a result felt very disconnected. She said, "I made a simple policy. I told my husband I would cook him dinner twice a week. It's amazing the benefits of just one little guideline. I let my husband know I want to be with him and still do well at the office. The policy eased my guilt when I was leaving work and my coworkers were still hard at it. The strategy helped me organize my thinking. I do want to balance work and family and deciding ahead of time what I will do takes the pressure off me."

Although a far cry from our parents' standards, dinner twice a week was just the ticket Denise's family needed. The strategist learned that she could endure the pain or establish polices.

## Living with No
Like many families, we do not answer the phone during dinner. It drove my teenagers crazy for only a little while. Now they don't even look up. It is not negotiable.

Declining to accept phone solicitations is another common limit. I am not against people who make their living on the telephone. I make a large part of my living talking to clients on the telephone—which is precisely why I don't want to receive a sales pitch at 8 P.M. when I am reading to my children or doing homework. When a call comes in and the voice says, "Hello, Mrs. LoVedi, La Veety, Mrs. Verd, how are you tonight?" I very politely say, "I'm sorry, we don't accept phone solicitations." Ninety-nine percent of the time, the solicitor says, "OK, thank you very much." Remember the guiding principle: every action should have more than one benefit? Because I don't accept phone solicitations, the telemarketers remove my name from the lists they sell each other. No one has called to clean my carpeting, side my house, or green my lawn for a couple of years now.

## I Do Not Sign Permission Slips in the Morning
I really like this policy, since one of my daily chores is waking up. No one has ever accused me of being sharp as a tack before 9 A.M. I do not, at 7 A.M., want to know about the field trip, the $6.68 entrance fee that must be on a money order or

notarized cashier's check, and the required sack lunch that will sit on a hot bus for eight hours growing God-knows-what-flesh-eating bacteria. I am only up to the challenge in the evening. You can't know how much this rule helped.

### Never More than a Grand

I have a policy. I never spend more than $1,000 without a twenty-four-hour wait. Have you ever been invited to one of those vacation time-share sales meetings? The ad promises you a free gift or a night's lodging if you agree to attend a sales presentation. My husband and I went to one in the beautiful Rocky Mountains. The salesperson could tell that we were "live ones" when we learned that we could trade the week to coordinate with our seminar locations. As our enthusiasm grew, I noticed he began using every closing technique in the book. At the end of his pitch I said sincerely, "We are very interested in this property. We have a policy. We never spend more than a thousand dollars without a twenty-four-hour wait, so we'll see you tomorrow."

He looked like a deer caught in headlights. What was he going to say—"Well, that's a stupid policy"?

I honored his efforts to sell us by letting him know we were interested and my hesitation was not a reflection on his selling ability. I was living my life according to my beliefs because I need time to think about major purchases without pressure. The next day we went back and closed the deal, certain we wouldn't suffer from buyer's remorse.

Bobbi Braun tried this technique. "My husband and I have both been using the phrase, 'I have a policy' and it's worked great. The insurance agent could only agree with me when I told him it was my policy never to sign anything until I had a week to look it over."

Sometimes people say to me, "But, Mary, what if it's a really good deal?" Then you can include in your directive the times when you'll amend your rules. For me, I have a long list of things I really want for $1,000, and if I am itching to spend that much money, I have ample opportunity!

> "Match every sock with something. Color, texture,
> and size is not important." (Erma Bombeck)

Many people have special instructions for the laundry. One woman with six children told me she has a rule that everyone in the family must wear the same color of clothes each day. Monday is blue, Tuesday is red, Wednesday is yellow, etc. Every day she does one load of the color du jour! That may seem a little restrictive, but let's face it, raising six kids isn't exactly a walk in the park, so if it works . . . Others believe clothes do not have feet, so they require their customers to actually return the basket to his or her room. Some cleaners insist, "If it is in the basket wrong side out, that is how you will get it back." A little policy-making goes a long way to making wash day easy.

## I'd Love to But . . .

Ron, a high school teacher, said he was the chairman of his department and was inundated (and stressed out) with requests to head committees and after-school clubs. In self-defense, he developed a policy. As chairman of the department, he agreed to head two additional activities. When approached with more requests, he simply said, "To be the best chairman I can be, I head two clubs each year. I would love to lead the Chess Club. Should I give up the school newspaper or the Spanish Club?"

## Sisterly Love

Leilani Guray, another teacher, used policies to get rid of excuses and improve her relationship with her sister. She wrote, "I have worked on my policy, which was to eat lunch with my sister once a week on the weekend. We are very close from the college years rooming together. Now that we are both starting careers, we rarely have the time to call each other, let alone get to see each other. After telling her that I made a personal policy to get together with her, she agreed we needed to connect again. Over the past month we met three times and enjoyed every second of it. We got to really talk about our personal lives. In just a month I am proud that I have worked on this issue that makes my life feel balanced. I can't wait to see what I do the rest of the year to feel more in harmony!"

## Speak Now or Forever Hold Your Peace

Marilyn Wirth and her neighbors of Marco Island, Florida, have a policy to handle the throng of houseguests that visit each year. As they drive over the bridge to the island, the host explains that all problems must be left on the bridge. The guests can pick them up again on their way out. The policy strictly forbids whining, blaming, criticizing, and grumbling. Conversations about aches and pains, detailed descriptions of a twelve-hour gallbladder surgery, and pity parties are illegal and subject to severe penalties. Sharing details about the daughter who never calls except when she needs money (she calls collect), the son who is having marital problems (you knew that woman wasn't good enough for him when they got married), and the grandchildren who never say thank you results in immediate expulsion from the island. In addition, Marilyn said, "The guests must be able to wash their own linens, make their own beds, and help with the cooking. And, of course," she added laughing, "I tell them to bring money!"

What fabulous policies. The people of Marco Island—God love 'em!

## Avoiding the Wedding Bell Blues

A friend of mine was getting ready to be married and asked my advice on how to have a stress-free wedding. She refused to elope, so I tried another idea. I asked her, "What do you think is the greatest source of anxiety?"

"My mother-in-law-to-be will arrive a few days before the wedding and stay with my fiancé. I don't know her well and I know Don will have a hard time with two women vying for his attention."

"Then you need a policy. Sit down with your fiancé and agree ahead of time how much time his mother gets and what you can expect."

The plan went into effect, everyone got their due, and there were no cake fights. (And I love a good cake fight.)

## Make It Stick

Every good negotiator will tell you if you're going to "win" you must get the other side to buy in to your idea or you are wasting your time. I remember every New Year's Eve my mother would announce there would be no eating in the family/living room. Every year her declaration lasted until halftime of the first bowl game when my five brothers would load up their plates and sit in front of the TV waiting for the second half to begin. My mother would say, "I thought I told you the new rule. No eating in the living room."

My brothers apologized and that was the last we heard of

the limitation until the next year. The carpet suffered greatly, as did my mother. There was just no mutual agreement.

Be prepared to stand your ground, explain until you are blue, and, if necessary, call in reinforcements. Sometimes I use a page out of my kids' own rule book and insist that "Jeremy's mom makes *him* do it." If the policy is grounded in good values and it promotes connection, stand firm. You may not get a standing ovation for insisting on compliance. You might have some people profusely questioning your wisdom, even when you strongly believe you know what is best. I think Erma Bombeck must have felt this way when she announced her policy: "The dog's business is EVERYONE'S business. Even when you don't see it, clean it up."

## THE NEW SOLUTION: POLICIES

*When we can't keep up, we have a choice. We can:*

| DISCONNECT | CONNECT |
|---|---|
| **Panic** | **Plan** |
| After-school activities, homework, the TV, the telephone, dinner—evenings at our house are like Grand Central Station! | It is time for a family meeting to set some limits. |
| **Feel powerless** | **Feel powerful** |
| This new project at work is going to kill me. I've worked six weekends in a row. | I will meet with my supervisor. Perhaps we can come up with a three-out-of-four weekend plan until this big project is finished. |

**Endure the pain**

Every year we go to my wife's relatives for vacation. I want to take the family on a sight-seeing tour.

**Establish policies**

Our new policy: We visit relatives in the even years and jointly pick out a vacation spot on the odd.

You already know how to use policies. You use them at work, at church or temple, and in your organizations. You accept the store's return policy, the insurance policy, and the IRS rules. Perhaps it is time to review your personal policies. They are not edicts, demands, or refusals. They are wisdom in management.

## MICROACTIONS

1. What are your current policies? Write out at least five. Are they working?
2. What new policies could you institute?
3. What would you gain if this policy went into effect?
4. What would you lose?
5. Make a list of the people it would affect. Who would you need to support you?
6. Ask your family or colleagues about their ideas.
7. What are the barriers to instituting your strategies?

## IN REAL LIFE

Dear Mary,

I am a mother, wife, and child of an aging parent, who also maintains a career as a scientist in research and development. I was particularly intrigued with your concept of using policies to achieve life balance. My extensive use of rules, especially at home, has often made me feel like a dictator. I followed your suggestion to change the verbiage to "Queen of Policies." I have found the use of policies in my home helps maintain some sense of organization and stability, while helping to eliminate the blame and guilt.

One of my favorite policies helps my family plan dinner for the upcoming week. Each member chooses a dinner menu for their assigned night of the week. For example, my husband chooses Monday dinners, my nine-year-old daughter chooses Tuesday, I pick Wednesday, and my six-year-old son picks on Thursday. I reserve the right to add a fruit or vegetable, but I have found that the kids have learned how to choose a balanced menu.

There are several additional policies that help to support the dinner menu policy. First, no one is allowed to complain about someone else's choice. This has helped to overcome the "I hate what we are having for dinner" syndrome. The "no complaining" policy has proved to be a challenge for my very vocal son, but it has also helped him, since he is very sensitive and doesn't like his choices criticized. The second support policy is: Friday night out! After a long week this is our family night to relax and have fun.

We also use policies to beat the morning rush since I am not a particularly relaxed person in the morning. One policy that helps me stay on track in the morning is Mom's Private Time. This is five to ten minutes to be alone in the bathroom each morning to style my hair and put on makeup. It was always extremely annoying to have someone knocking or loitering outside when I was already getting near the spin point. With this policy I no longer have to even shut the bathroom door. The kids know I will be available to answer questions, tie shoes, or fix a ponytail when I am ready for work.

Having policies at home has also helped me to maintain a better focus at work. The policies keep me connected to the people I love the most and the things that are important. This allows me to place my attention on the priorities and activities of my job.

Thanks for making a connection in my life.

Mary Jo Meyer
Research Scientist
Kimberly-Clark Corporation

# CHAPTER 10

# Disband the Camps

Jerry Scott and Rick Kirkman, BABY BLUES, copyright © 1996,
Reprinted with special permission of King Features Syndicate.

Human beings are the only creatures who are able to
behave irrationally in the name of reason.

—*Ashley Montagu*

Just as Betty Crocker got updated to reflect modern
society's view of women, we need a new role model
for connection. The first step in that direction is to look carefully at our current models. My research suggests that we have
divided our world into two major camps, male and female.
Each of these camps is subdivided into smaller camps. Let's
take a look at the female division first.

# THE FEMALE CAMPS
"I have a uterus and a brain and they both work."
(Former Congresswoman Pat Schroeder)

There are four major female camps.

## 1. The stay-at-home-mom camp

You know these women: they are those formerly bright, vivacious, creative women who develop brain mush from too much daytime television. They are experts on what is happening to Erica on *All My Children*, their kids develop the Hurried Child Syndrome, and critics tell us these poor women have no libido.

## 2. Full-time-working-mother coalition

You know these women, too. They are the harried, hassled ones, seen at the grocery store at midnight buying frozen pizzas and rice cakes. Their children like their day care mothers the best, and some evidence suggests their children will grow up to be mass murderers or, at the very least, shave their heads and pass out books at the airport for a donation. These pathetic women also have no libido.

## 3. Part-time-flex-time-job-sharing crowd

You can't miss these ladies. They are so used to doing two things at once that they paint their nails while they drive, review memos while they carpool, and mentally make out grocery lists while they make love. (Sometimes the grocery list takes longer.) You can't give them anything important to do at work because they're gone half the time. You can't really consider them very good parents because they're gone the other half too. They do, I understand, have a libido . . . but only two and a half days a week.

## 4.  Career-Woman society

These single, married, or divorced childless females own dozens of Bill Blass dresses, white sofas, and glass-topped coffee tables. (You know, the kind with the pointed edges just waiting to poke some poor kid's eye out.) They have perfectly manicured nails. These women are *never too tired for sex*. Critics charge some are a little egotistical and tend to be workaholics. They have slightly swollen heads from continuously ramming it into the glass ceiling. Despite these criticisms, they are, let me remind you, *never too tired for sex*.

## Mini Camps

There are many small subdivisions within each camp. The Empty Nesters, for example, are often lonely, needy, and prone to hot flashes. The Adult College Student slows down the class with inane questions that aren't even going to be on the test. And don't get me started commenting on the retirees who create long lines at noon when busy important people are trying to do their banking.

## Do Not Pass Go, Go Directly to Jail

Can you imagine someone writing these critiques? In these politically correct times, do you know how much trouble you could get into? Do you know how many people you might offend, or how much time you could spend in jail? The fact remains: the camps exist. We created them out of a need to defend ourselves. Society told women they were free to choose any role in life. There just wasn't any support for that choice. Uncertain about the validity of our selection and threatened by other women's preferences, we all dug in our heels and declared that our camp was the Right One and all those other camps, why, they were made up of unhappy people with ruined sex lives who were raising misguided, unhealthy children.

It is time to disband the camps! They no longer serve any useful purpose. Perhaps at one time they helped us. They gave us strength and insight so we could carefully evaluate how each group managed. With little support for any of the camps, it was natural that we banded together with like minds.

I have wonderful news! I have carefully researched the latest studies and I can prove which camp is best for all women. At last we will know once and for all.

## Stay-at-Home Moms Are the Best

According to Yanklovich, Clancy, and Schulman, 28 percent of working women wanted to quit their jobs and put more energy into homemaking. Fifty-six percent of working women said that having enough money would get them to quit. In this survey, less than 50 percent of women thought mothers should also have a career. In addition, we are all aware of the enormous amount of literature supporting the mother-child bond, especially in those tender formative years. The data are in. Women want to go home and it's the best thing for their families. All women should join this camp.

## Full-Time Career Moms Are the Best

According to Boston University and others, work is a positive for mothers and children alike. Both mothers and children, according to a University of California study, have higher self-esteem and fewer health problems. Working mothers are happier and less depressed than their stay-at-home sisters, and according to Harvard University, their children have a less sex-stereotyped view of the world and fewer behavior problems. Research very clearly shows that women want to go to work and it's the best thing for their families. All women should join this camp.

## Flex-Time-Part-Time-Job-Sharing Moms Are the Best

According to the executive recruitment firm of Robert Half International, 78 percent of people prefer a flexible work schedule. Telecommuting has been growing by leaps and bounds. According to Link Resources, home-based workers actually accomplish 10 to 20 percent more than people in the office. Millions of women run home-based businesses. The corporate world, although slow to change, is finally addressing work and family issues. Johnson & Johnson, for only the third time in the history of the company, changed their creed to add the statement "we must be mindful of ways to help our employees meet their family obligations." J & J, a leader in family-friendly companies, which has a clear commitment to on-site day care, just began a program to help their employees find in-home day care as well. Studies show companies lose millions of dollars each year due to absenteeism caused by family-care problems. Flex-time produces fierce employee loyalty and financial savings for both employee and employer. Numbers don't lie. Women want alternative work schedules and it is the best thing for their families. All women should join this camp.

## Career Women Are the Best

There is no research on career women. White sofas, great sex; who would research that? Just kidding. Actually, the research shows very clearly that the price to reach the top is a heavy one, that some women are fed up and are bailing out. It also reveals women showing up in boardrooms, women-owned businesses skyrocketing to success, and millions of females loving their careers. Without a doubt the data clearly show this to be far superior to the others. All women should join this camp.

## A Rose Is a Rose

Here's my favorite piece of research: Lois Hoffman, Ph.D., from the University of Michigan, surveyed fifty years of research and found out that whether mothers work or not, children don't differ. John Ellis, of East Tennessee State, conducted a study of mothers' employment on children's behavior and found out that, regardless of the mother's employment status, the children's moods and behavior didn't change. What does this mean? It means that if you have a two-year-old and they throw a fit at 6 P.M., it doesn't mean you are a stay-at-home mom and you are smothering the child; it doesn't mean you are a full-time mom and you are neglecting the child; and it doesn't mean you are a flex-time mom and you are confusing the child. It means that at 6 P.M., two-year-olds throw fits!

## And Last but Not Least

Cornell University tracked 313 women over three decades and concluded that the more roles a woman has *by choice*, the higher her self-esteem and the better her health.

## Disband the Camps

So you see, research very clearly shows that the choice doesn't matter. What matters is that *you* like your choice. What matters is that you feel your choice helps you connect with yourself, your family, your friends, and your God. What matters is that you feel that your life is in balance. And that choice can be just about anything.

P.S.
There is one other camp to disband. The single-mother camp. Three days before Christmas a friend of mine, a divorced mother of three school-aged children, was fired from her job of twenty years. She was on probation for tardiness because her son's day care did not open until 6:30 A.M. and with traffic and other delays she sometimes clocked in at 7:10. Late one time too many, she was fired on the spot.

I am not implying we can all show up late for work. But I wonder if this is an outdated Cleaver principle in action. In the mythical "good old days" chronic tardiness meant you were disorganized, lazy, or uncommitted to your job. Now it might mean we need to review the rules and work together to find solutions to the real problem. Of course, this doesn't apply to just single parents. They may, however, lead the way in teaching us new ways of thinking as we attempt to unravel this camp.

## Taking the First Step Toward Reuniting

OK, you say. I am ready to disband the camps. But how do I start? The easiest way is to recognize how we benefit each other. For example, the stay-at-home mom doesn't just stay at home. She's the homeroom mother planning activities for your child, grandchild, or niece or nephew. She's the hospice volunteer, the organizer of community programs, and the Cub Scout leader. The stay-at-home mom benefits me and my family.

The working mom doesn't just earn a paycheck. She's making great strides at eliminating the glass ceiling, outlawing sexual harassment, and instituting policies that are socially and environmentally sound. She's striving to create a more humane planet for all of us. Even if we choose to stay home, our daughters and daughters-in-law might not. We have the working mom to thank for pioneering this role. The working mother benefits me and my family.

The alternate-work-schedule mom doesn't just juggle. She's leading the way in exploring new ways to balance work and family, ways that the rest of us might someday use. She's covering for you by feeding Jell-O to your "home with the flu" child. She's rearranging her schedule to accommodate yours. The flex-time mom benefits me and my family.

The career woman. Oh, boy. This is the camp I had to disband. I used to think, "She only has to take care of herself and she can't balance her life. What's wrong with her? If I only had to think of myself, I could do it with one hand tied behind my back!"

What an arrogant and erroneous attitude! First of all, the late Mother Teresa may have been ahead of us, but the rest of us are back together in a pack. Married, single, divorced, childless, or Old Mother Hubbard, we all face the same universal and timeless issues. The career woman needs holidays off to have a whole life, too.

I finally recognized that the career woman has a lot to teach me. My older career female colleague can offer me her wisdom gained through years of experience, warn me of the pitfalls ahead, and teach me new ways to think. The younger career woman reminds me of things I sometimes forget in my day full of car pools, soccer practices, and homework. She invites me to lunch at that wonderful new French restaurant, one I wouldn't have discovered until their fifth anniversary. She shops with me and, diplomatically, steers me in the direction of the latest fashion. She quotes good advice from the latest business book, when the last book I read is *The Berenstain Bears*. The career woman definitely benefits me and my family.

We have so much to give one another. Begin the new solution and start disbanding those camps today. If you're a stay-at-home mom or flex-time mom, double that soup recipe while the kids are napping or are at school and take it to a working mother. It's worth its weight in gold. Take an extra car pool turn. There is nothing that will balance your life more than balancing someone else's.

If you're a working mom, call your stay-at-home sister and offer to watch her kids on a Saturday so she can have lunch with a friend, take a class at the local college, or (you know the most coveted of all) go to the grocery store without the kids. If you have someone in your office who has been asking for an alternate work schedule, reconsider and get more information. It might be more beneficial than you think. And give flex-time people important roles in your company. Studies show that full-time people really *work* only for thirty-five hours a week. The rest of the time is spent socializing and daydreaming. If someone is willing to give up those distractions and really focus, tap into that talent.

Support the career woman, as well. She may not have sick kids, car pools, and day care deadlines, but her life-balance concerns are just as valid and urgent. Rethink your opinions of all the subdivisions as well. You will discover the women in those mini camps have gifts to offer us, too.

And finally, we have to drop the disapproval of the single parent. Ask her how you can help. Could you look in on her child after school until she gets home? Can you take her son to gymnastic practice on Thursdays? Can you help her explore a plan for sick-child day care so she doesn't have to call in sick, too? Remember, any of us could become a single mom in the blink of an eye.

As my Hawaiian friends remind me: *"Ikaika Na Wahine I Ka Lokahi"*—The strength of women is in their unity!

## THE MALE CAMPS

Jerry Scott and Rick Kirkman, BABY BLUES, copyright © 1992.
Reprinted with special permission of King Features Syndicate.

Let's take a look at the male groups.

### 1. The traditionalist

He knows his role, a woman's place, and how to coach Little League.

### 2. The transitionist

Like Mel Gibson, Kevin Costner, and Tim Allen, who vacuum in boxer shorts while watching ESPN.

### 3. The liberated, New Age guy of the nineties

Like Phil Donahue clones, these men insist they actually enjoy changing dirty diapers. They'll eat fondue, go to chick flicks, and smoke stinky cigars on boys' night out.

In some ways, I think it is easier for men to break up their groups. Perhaps it is because they are not as entrenched, as they flow from unit to unit under different circumstances. Maybe it is because men are ready to change. Faith Popcorn, considered by many to be the premiere trend guru, predicts that "emancipation" will be one of the top trends to watch. She describes the new male as "unshackled from the bondage of machismo. Liberated from being distant, disconnected, remote, unromantic, analytical, forever Strictly Business."

We see the "new male" when David Williams was fined $100,000 by the Houston Oilers for missing the game but chose to be at the birth of his child anyway. We see it when 3.5 million men now stay home while their wives work. We see it when there is a baby-changing station in the men's restroom. Men are definitely "changing," albeit some slower than others.

In other ways it may be harder for men to adapt. Role expectations have changed with lightning quickness compared to other generations. Consider this: What if when the Beaver was born, Ward had said to June's obstetrician, "I don't want to stay in the waiting room and hand out cigars. I want to be in the delivery room and cut the umbilical cord." Everyone would have labeled him a sicko! Now imagine your dad making that request when you were born? For most of our fathers, it would have been a very inappropriate request. Yet one short generation later we want his son to love the idea. I'm not saying men shouldn't adapt. I am simply saying that if a man is trying, all of us—men and women alike—must support him. The magnitude of change is not easy on any of us.

Jerry Scott and Rick Kirkman, BABY BLUES, copyright © 1992,
Reprinted with special permission of King Features Syndicate.

## The He versus She Camp

The emotional and psychological differences between men and women has been a hot topic of discussion for several years. From Deborah Tannen's *You Just Don't Understand* to John Gray's *Men Are from Mars, Women Are from Venus*, we are in essence trying to understand one another so we can disband the "he versus she" camps. Two studies changed my views about men and women.

### Shockingly True

The first experiment was an animal research study, duplicated by generations of psychology students, that shows "mothering" is one of the deepest needs a female has.

The experiment goes like this. There are two metal boxes separated by an electrified grid. A rat is deprived of something and put in Box One. The item it is deprived of is put in Box Two (the Goal Box). For example, a hungry or thirsty rat will have food or water in Box Two. A mother rat will have her newborn pups in the second box. A rat deprived of air will find oxygen in the Goal Box. The researcher opens the door to Box One and measures the number and intensity of electrical shocks that the rat is willing to endure in order to get to the goal in Box Two.

Animal rights aside (I don't think they do this experiment anymore), the results are fascinating. Rats deprived of air sustained the most electrical shocks to get to the Goal Box. Mother rats endured almost as many to get to their pups. Water and food came in third and fourth.

An even more fascinating result was that male rats did not race across electrical shocks to get to their babies. However, researchers found that a nurturing need could be created in male rats by injecting them with female hormones.

When I read this experiment, I cried, "Eureka!" It explained so much. When I anguished over leaving my sick child, when I yearned to stay home, when I felt stabs of guilt for traveling on business, I was, as Joyce Brothers said, "simply obeying my primitive need to nurture, listening to my universal Preportant Needs." And when my husband was *not* anguishing over leaving the little munchkins with a baby-sitter, it did not mean he did not love them. We are just wired differently. This is not evidence suggesting men should shirk their duty of staying home with sick kids, finding baby-sitters, or rearranging their schedules to accommodate ballet lessons. It means I can stop being angry with my husband because he doesn't get *upset* about it. He would not streak across an electrical grid just to fix the kids a peanut butter and jelly sandwich. (Unless, of course, I sneaked into the bedroom while he was sleeping and injected him with female hormones. The thought has crossed my mind.)

Oh Romeo, Romeo, How Dost Thou Make
Thy Bed?

Here is the other study that will help disband the he/she camp. Two sociologists from the University of Illinois, Jean Huger and Glenn Spitz, studied 1,360 married couples. The researchers found that how much money each spouse earned had no effect on thoughts of divorce. Neither did attitudes about gender roles. What was significant? The amount of housework a wife saw her husband doing! The more housework he shared, the less likely she was to think of divorce.

Husbands, listen up! Doing the housework has little to do with dust and everything to do with respect. Wipe the counters. Throw in a load of towels. Fix dinner. Don't view it as housework. Consider it an insurance run for a secure marriage. (And let them see you sweat!)

## THE NEW SOLUTION:
## DISBAND THE CAMPS

*When we can't keep up, we have a choice. We can:*

### DISCONNECT

**Cling to the old role models**
I have to pick up my kids at day care. John doesn't have kids. Let him stay late.

**Find fault**
Melissa's mom travels a lot and misses nearly every ballet recital. I just don't see how she can do that to her daughter.

**Reject each other's choice**
Can you believe Frank adopted an older child? He's not even married!

### CONNECT

**Create new role models**
We've all got lives. How can we work this out fairly?

**Find ways to support**
I bet she hates missing out on the excitement. Maybe she'd like me to film the recital for her with my camcorder.

**Recognize the benefits of each choice**
What a wonderful opportunity for my kids to watch a nurturing father.

Ban mommy wars, male bashing, and ruined sex lives. Let's put our weapons down and make a genuine effort to reach out and connect with one another. No one has cornered the market on stress.

## MICROACTIONS

1. What camp or club are you in? Is it the right group for you right now? If yes, why? If not, why not? What division would you like to be in?

2. What camp do you need to disband? How could you begin?

3. Think of a recipe that easily doubles. Take half of it to someone who will smile from ear to ear and probably kiss you.

4. If you know how, offer to help a single mom with that squeaky garage door, leaking pipe, or broken fence.

5. Think how your life would change if you were in someone else's shoes. How would you feel if you were a part-time employee, a full-time supervisor, a new adoptive parent? What if you suddenly became a single dad?

6. Tell someone, "You are a *good parent.*" It is a rarely used phrase.

7. Invite a single person to a holiday celebration.

## IN REAL LIFE

Dear Mary,

I have felt compelled to write to you since listening to your audiotape, "June Cleaver Never Fried Bacon in a Bill Blass Dress," which I received from a friend who heard the obvious desperation in my voice. My life undoubtedly lacked life balance, and I had no clear vision as to how I could change that. . . . I wasn't sure I even had a choice. Let me explain.

I am a forty-one-year-old mother of a two-and-a-half-year-old little boy. Married for fifteen years before being blessed with our son, I was a career woman with a closet *full* of designer clothes and a home full of "pretty" things —right down to the white sofa (honestly!). Let me just say this . . . I have friends who still get a good laugh when we relive the conversation of my telling them not only that I was pregnant, *but with a boy!* I mean my lifestyle and white sofa were not designed to accommodate a child.

I had absolutely no idea that I was the description of the Career Woman Camp. To be honest, I never really thought about camps. . . . I was too busy getting through each demanding day of deadlines, meetings, and the journey through Corporate America. Boy, was my head in the sand! I can even recall a conversation I had with my husband as we were getting ready to go to the athletic club to work out. I told him, *with conviction,* that life won't change much once the baby arrives! I actually believed that my experiences, organization, and planning skills would save me from all the stories I was told.

Since there was not one ounce of reality in my thinking, things absolutely changed. All of a sudden, the designer suits held much less value, my deadlines now included 3 A.M. feedings, and my journey through Corporate America stopped in my son's sweet little room. I felt and still feel such peace in that room. You see, my son arrived in this world almost two months early, weighing in at just 3.5 pounds, but a little fighter. My new journey now took me through emotions and "innate" needs that I never anticipated. All of a sudden I wanted to be a "stay-at-home mom," but I didn't know how to be . . . all I knew was what I had been for so long. It took me a while, but I finally learned that I do have choices, and it is OK to pursue them.

The greatest realization was the importance of connecting with the people around me who have already mastered the wonder of "choices" and to appreciate the value of allowing people to help. All those years of independence . . . the I-can-do-this-on-my-own era was history! I learned to ask for help and receive it willingly, and in return, feel the need to extend my help to others.

My life is now much more fulfilling than it was prior to September 7, 1993. My career is now a three-day work week—twenty-four vs. sixty hours. My home is still filled with a lot of pretty things, but with a lot of bright red, blue, and green accents (if you know what I mean). The white sofa still exists, but for very different reasons and with much less importance. . . . It's called life balance.

Thank you so much for your encouragement and vision.

With warmest regards,

Toni L. Shorthouse

PART IV

# *Connecting*
## with the
# Big Picture

# CHAPTER 11

# Keeping Company with the Wise

When I am dead
I hope it may be said:
His sins were scarlet
but his books were read.
—*Hilaire Belloc*

Ever read a passage that just pierces your soul? I was reading an article by Brian Tracy and stopped in my tracks. Brian, a leading authority on success and personal achievement, wrote, "A great many people do not read very much. According to the American Booksellers, in 1991, fully 80 percent of American families did not buy or read a single book. Fifty-eight percent of Americans never read a nonfiction book from cover to cover after they finish high school. The average American reads less than one book per year. In fact, according to a Gallup study of the most successful men and women in America, reading one non-fiction book per month will put you in the top one percent of living Americans."

Does that blow you away? At first I didn't believe it. But as I have traveled and recommended books to my audiences, CEOs, secretaries, bank presidents, teachers, nurses, managers

—well-educated people from all walks of life have confessed they hadn't read a nonfiction book for over ten years. I have to admit I did not read very much in the years I was chasing toddlers and keeping the wash from piling to the ceiling. When it dawned on me that I needed to bombard my mind with good ideas—that the answers to my life-balance problems were in books—my first question was, "OK, so *which* books?" I didn't want to read just anything. Couldn't someone direct me to the best books?

By accident I came across a list in *Parade* magazine entitled, "The top ten most influential books." The authors of the list surveyed Book of the Month Club members and Library of Congress users and asked them, "What one book most influenced your life?" The resultant top ten list (there are actually thirteen because four tied for the last spot) seemed like a good place for me to start.

And what a list it is! (See page 191.) My favorite book on the list is *Gift from the Sea* by Anne Morrow Lindbergh. If I could have authored any book, I'd have chosen hers. She so beautifully and accurately describes the stages of a woman's life and the joys and trials that go with each one. The most amazing aspect of the book is that she wrote it in 1955! You will swear she looked into your soul and wrote it yesterday—just for you! I suppose it could be classified as a woman's book (I urge all my male friends to give it to their wives), but I have been pleasantly surprised at the number of men who had read it and described it as "profound." I love to mention the book in my seminars because I can see eyes gleam from those that know the book. Ann T. McKennis, an operating room nurse from The Woodlands, Texas, wrote,

Dear Mary,

*Gift from the Sea* has always been my favorite book. It was given to me in 1958 as a high school graduation gift. I have lost track of how many times I have read it and how many copies I have given as gifts. It should be in every woman's library.

I have a tattered copy that stays on my bedside table. It is the copy I carry when I travel to the beach. Every year, a dear friend and I escape to the seashore for a couple of days to renew ourselves and find balance in our lives. This started when our children were small and we could only be gone for six or seven hours. She paints and I write poetry, meditate, and read *Gift from the Sea*. It has become our annual commune with the sea.

How wonderful to have been able to write a book forty years ago that still truly speaks to a woman's soul. Anne Morrow Lindbergh states, "woman must come of age by herself" . . . and how beautifully she teaches us.

## Top Ten Most Influential Books

1. *The Bible*
2. *Atlas Shrugged*
   Ayn Rand
3. *The Road Less Traveled*
   M. Scott Peck
4. *To Kill a Mockingbird*
   Harper Lee
5. *The Lord of the Rings*
   J. R. R. Tolkien
6. *Gone With the Wind*
   Margaret Mitchell

7. *How to Win Friends and Influence People*
   Dale Carnegie
8. *The Book of Mormon*
9. *The Feminine Mystique*
   Betty Friedan
*10. *Gift from the Sea*
   Anne Morrow Lindbergh
   (It is also on tape, read by the late Claudette Colbert. She has the most calming, lovely voice.)
*10. *Man's Search for Meaning*
   Viktor Frankl
*10. *Passages*
   Gail Sheehy
*10. *When Bad Things Happen to Good People*
   Harold Kushner

There are obviously countless inspirational books. I'd like to recommend a few of my favorites that have received rave reviews from my audiences.

*Chocolate for a Woman's Soul: 77 Stories to Feed Your Spirit and Warm Your Heart*
Kay Allenbaugh
If you can read this book without being touched, call 911 immediately, because you have died and no one told you. The true stories are about the magic, miracles, perfect timing, and insights these sixty-eight female authors experienced. You won't be able to put it down.

*Tongue Fu! How to Deflect, Disarm, and Defuse Any Verbal Conflict*
Sam Horn

* These books all tied for the last spot.

Ever have verbal conflict? I thought so. If you want fast, easy-to-learn skills that will dramatically improve your relationship with your spouse, help you deal with sibling rivalry, get your boss to say "yes," and handle that rude customer with grace and style—this is the book for you. It should be required reading for human beings. Tongue Fu, the verbal form of martial arts, teaches us "words to lose and words to use." For example, I learned I can avoid a lot of conflict by losing the word *should* and replacing it with *in the future*. Instead of telling my kids what they *should* have done (after the fact when my advice can't possibly be utilized), I can say, "In the future, I'd like you to ask me before you take my new bedspread on the camping trip." The book is full of simple communication ideas that really work, ways to avoid disconnecting, and strategies to make connecting easy. My family has definitely benefited. Maybe the bedspread never did come clean but, I must say, we are better at communicating. Even old dogs can learn new verbal tricks.

Check out Sam's other books: *Concrete Confidence: A 30-Day Program for an Unshakable Foundation of Self-Assurance*, and *ConZentrate!: 101 Ways to Pay Attention to What's Really Important*. You will be glad you did!

*The Alchemist*
Paulo Coelho
This award-winning sleeper of a book is a marvelous fable about following your dream. (It has sold over nine million copies worldwide.) A little boy takes you on an unforgettable journey, reminding us how to find our treasures in life. You will see yourself on every page. Read it to the end. The punch line is a keeper. (There is more than one book with this same title. Be sure you get the one by Coelho.)

*Small Miracles: Everyday Coincidences from Everyday Life*
Yitta Halberstam and Judith Levanthal
This wonderful book is a collection of over sixty stories about remarkable coincidences—many of them small miracles to be sure. I started reading this book on the plane one day and was annoyed a few hours later when we landed because I didn't want to stop. If you believe that "there are no coincidences," this is the book for you.

*Don't Sweat the Small Stuff . . . and It's All Small Stuff*
Richard Carlson
This number-one *New York Times* bestseller is a collection of one hundred short essays describing simple ways to keep the little things from taking over your life. One reviewer wrote, "Like Stairmasters, oat bran, and other things that are good for you, the meditations take discipline. Even so, some of the strategies are kind of fun." The writing is inspiring, and if we all followed Dr. Carlson's advice, the world would be a better place.

*Words That Heal*
One August I gave my favorite daily meditational book to my friend Stan during his visit. Upon his return to Durango, he put it on his bookshelf. In October, his girlfriend's eighteen-year-old son was killed in a car accident. He and Debra returned to us for a visit at Thanksgiving.

As we were saying our good-byes, Debra turned to me and said, "I want to thank you for the book you gave us."

"Oh, sure, it was my pleasure. I'm glad you enjoyed it."

"No," she said, "you don't understand. It was about a week after Jesse's death and I was home alone, having a very bad day. I decided reading might help take my mind off my loss for a while. I went to our bookshelf and found this book. I'd never seen it before. I wondered how it got there. At random, I opened the book and looked down. Unbelievably, the topic was tragedy. I read the passage and I want you to know it was those three paragraphs that got me through the day. Thank you so very much."

After they left, I retrieved my copy and read the words that had meant so much to Debra. The story was about a mother sobbing over the loss of her child, wondering why she should have to endure such pain and asking the Buddha for guidance.

We can only imagine what Debra felt as she read those paragraphs in her dark hour. She reminded me to never underestimate the power of words to help us connect and find peace.

## Reading Will Change Your Mind

I became an avid bibliophile by changing the way I viewed reading. Remember the commercial for Brylcreem, a men's hair lotion, with their motto, "A little dab'll do ya"? (You are dating yourself if you do.) It is a wonderful motto for readers, too. Just a little dab of reading goes a long way. I used to say I couldn't read because I didn't have enough time. I thought I had to read the whole book or I would not benefit.

How wrong I was. I read Price Pritchett's book *New Work Habits for a Radically Changing World* and found the sentence that changed my whole attitude about losing my job. He penned the words I needed to read—on page 39!

Rapid organizational change guarantees us that almost everybody is going to carry some battle scars in the years to come. You can be bitter about how your career gets affected, or you can demonstrate your ability to take a punch. You can carry a grudge to your grave, or you can "get over it."

It didn't take a whole book to put my life in order. "Demonstrate your ability to take a punch." That was all the insight I needed.

## The Only Time I Have to Read Is at Night and I Fall Asleep

I used to believe this myth, too. My audiences taught me how to read at lunch, on fifteen-minute breaks, on the Stairmaster, in the tub when I get home from work—instead of watching TV. They convinced me to "read" audiotaped books in the car while I waited for soccer practice or while I jogged. One man goodnaturedly chided me, "If you were being paid by the word you'd find a way to grab a few minutes."

Touché.

## I Only Have Time for My Professional Reading

Staying current in your field is vital. I don't want a doctor who hasn't browsed *The New England Journal of Medicine* in years yet can quote Howard Stern's latest book. But rethink the term "professional reading." The world is a pretty complicated place. I doubt we can read just one topic and know everything we need to be successful. We'll be delighted with the crossover possibilities.

Mary Jones of Lafayette, Louisiana, an OR nurse, called to say this was her experience. "When I heard you describe the professional who hadn't read a book in ten years I sat there thinking, 'That's me!' I made a commitment to read just one of your recommendations and I am calling to tell you I am really hooked on reading. I can't stop! I get ideas I can use at work, at home—everywhere."

## Getting "Paid" by the Word

Wouldn't it be great if someone really would pay us by the word? Well, in a sense we do earn something with every phrase and every story. We get the answers to our problems, an open door to incredible adventure and understanding, and the pathway to intriguing insights. Norman Vincent Peale said, "Always be on the lookout for the big idea that will change your life."

I bet he meant, "Read."

## THE NEW SOLUTION:
## READ

*When we can't keep up we have a choice. We can:*

| DISCONNECT | CONNECT |
| --- | --- |
| **Read to lament** <br> The paper depresses me, the tabloids are full of lies. There is nothing good to read. | **Love to read** <br> I joined a book club. I can't wait to start the new selection. |
| **Read nothing and gain nothing** <br> I haven't the time or the inclination to read. I wouldn't know where to start. | **Read a little and gain a lot** <br> I'm going to get a quote book, put it on the nightstand, and read it aloud to my spouse before we go to sleep. |

| Reinvent the wheel to solve your problems | Research how others have solved your problems |
|---|---|
| I keep making the same mistakes. Life is not getting any better. | I found a stack of books on the issue in the library. It's reassuring to know I'm not the only one and there is help. |

Dave Barry suggests we give people an additional tax exemption for every book report they attach to their income tax returns. I like the idea. Until Senator Barry gets that bill passed, perhaps you'll make yourself a promise to read more. You might just find yourself in that top 1 percent of living Americans.

## MICROACTIONS

1. Make a list of everything you have read in the last month. Include trade journals, newspapers, magazines, paperbacks, even the back of the cereal box. What do you notice about your reading habits?
2. Read one paragraph a day in something that you don't normally read.
3. Ask someone what they like to read.
4. Go to the bookstore and just look around.
5. Donate a book to the library.
6. Put a book on the nightstand.
7. Go to a book signing.

## IN REAL LIFE

Dear Mary,

Not too long ago, my husband (whose reading tastes are confined pretty much to true-life crime, gangster books, and sci-fi) decided to read *In Cold Blood*. I had read it years ago but had forgotten much of it, so I picked it up and read it when he was done. Afterward, we had what we thought would be a short discussion of our impressions of the book. But instead, the topic kept cropping up for days. And we discovered that we liked these book discussions. Now we are looking for other books that interest us both so we can discuss them in our private "book club." Please send me your list of favorite books.

Thank you again for an interesting and thought-provoking discussion.

Sincerely,

Lisa Gough

Arlington, Virginia

# CHAPTER 12

# You Can Have It All

If you think you can do it all, be it all, have it all, snap out of it! That much success must be fatal because we've never met a person that lucky who's survived.
—*Marcia Byalick and Linda Saslow*
The Three-Career Couple

You can have it "all"! Now aren't you glad you bought this book! For the low, low price of one book you can learn how to get your heart's desire. I'm serious. I have to think that I can have it all because the minute you tell me that I can't, my first question is, "So which part don't I get?" I doubt we can keep our lives in balance believing we are living in chronic deprivation. We have to know we can have it all.

If we are going to solve our life-balance problems with connection, we must begin to think in a different way about what we want and need. "Having it all" has taken on negative connotations because we have allowed everyone else to tell us what the phrase means. This is ridiculous. For those of you who wear panty hose, you know that no matter what the package says, one size *does not* fit all.

Life balance is exactly the same way. You must determine

what kind of life makes you, as Dr. Lawrence LeShan says, glad to get up in the morning and glad to go to bed at night.

## What Does It Look Like?

When I ask people what their pictorial view of "balance through connection" is, they often mention old-fashioned scales with each side in equal proportion. If that is your view, may I simply say: Lotsaluck.

I can't imagine how any of us could achieve that—much less maintain it. I also don't believe that's what we are really after, anyway. I am certainly not looking for everything to be "equal."

The figure below represents my ideal life balance:

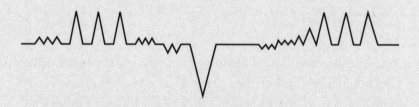

The peaks represent the highs of life. I love the rushes and the exhilaration of going after them. They might be the thrill of reaching a much-sought-after goal, getting married, or experiencing childbirth. Or it might be the moment-to-moment highs of watching my son score a soccer goal on his birthday, receiving a wonderful letter, or finding the perfect dress 50 percent off. I definitely need some euphoria to keep my life in sync.

But what happens to people who like a lot of highs? Yep. We have lows. We risk and we fail, and we risk and we fail, over and over again. Sometimes it looks like we'll never learn.

The lows almost seem a prerequisite if we are to soar to great heights. After each plunge I need to return to the baseline. I take a deep breath, brush myself off, and then I want to get right back after it. I'll probably fall off again and again. To me, the falls are worth it if it means I can get back to those highs.

### Down in the Dumps

Do you see the big dip in the middle of the graph? Sometimes you can do everything right and it still doesn't work. None of us is immune. Bad things happen and we have no control over them. When those events occur, I know that to get re-connected, I need to spend more time at the baseline, reassessing what happened, healing and reenergizing. When my strength returns I can take off again, albeit a little slower initially. I want to get up in the morning looking forward to something and I want to go to bed with that "good tired" feeling that comes from exhilaration. For me, this is connection.

### Another view

This is the life-balance graph of one of my friends, Sally.

She likes everything nice and smooth and calm. Sally's idea of having it all is serenity. She stays poised by staying as close to the baseline as possible. She doesn't like lofty ambitions; they make her nervous. She despises the setbacks; they make her depressed. When I look at her graph, I think, "For crying out loud! This is a picture of boredom! I've seen people near death with more exciting life-balance graphs than this." And when she looks at my life balance graph she says, "You know, Mary, there are prescription drugs to control this sort of thing."

A woman in my seminar drew the graph below as her ideal.

She said she liked things pretty calm and easygoing but also liked looking forward to something. She said, "My graph made me realize I really didn't want to have a series of exciting events without a break. I forgave myself for not being more ambitious. I realized I intuitively knew what I needed for life balance and I automatically paced myself."

A man told me his graph was a star, with each point representing an important part of his life. He understood that he couldn't have highs in every category at the same time. Instead he would experience that success, return to the center, and then plan for victory in another area of his life. He said he realized from graphing his ideal that he got out of balance most often when he tried to be in more than one star point at a time.

## The One and Only
Don't let everyone else tell you how to "draw" your life. It will be one-of-a-kind, as it should be.

What does your ideal life-balance graph look like? Draw it in
the space below.

```
┌─────────────────────────────────────────────┐
│                    IDEAL                      │
│                                               │
│                                               │
│                                               │
│                                               │
└─────────────────────────────────────────────┘
```

Now let's look at what life you are really living. Draw what
your current life balance looks like.

```
┌─────────────────────────────────────────────┐
│                   REALITY                     │
│                                               │
│                                               │
│                                               │
└─────────────────────────────────────────────┘
```

Notice any discrepancies? When my life gets out of whack I
look at what I am supposed to be doing to keep everything in
place and what I am *actually* doing. For example, if I am just
getting over a major disappointment, I know I should be
spending time at the baseline healing and rejuvenating. If I am
instead blindly going after thrills to avoid facing my feelings
or in a feeble attempt to make myself feel good, I can tell from
my graph why I am out of sorts and what I must do to get
back in line. My graph will tell me that I need to grieve or be
angry, or cry and scream. It will show me that now is not the
time to take on big projects or travel or remodel the kitchen.
It will remind me that I need to ask myself, "Who do I need
to connect to right now?"

Know what kind of life you want and then focus on living it
that way. If highs are your idea of balance, go for it. If tranquility is a better way for you, don't apologize to your adrenaline
junkie friends for it. One size does not fit all.

## All Versus Everything

You can also use your graph to understand the difference between All and Everything. I firmly believe you can have it
All. And I also firmly believe you cannot have Everything.
The comedian Stephen Wright says "You can't have *everything*. Where would you *put* it?" If you make that picture,
you realize how ridiculous it is to strive for Everything. The
difference between All and Everything is this: Having it All
connects you with yourself, your family, other people, or your
spirituality. Striving to have Everything disconnects you. You
might get it but the price is so high you end up more out of
balance.

Look at my graph and Sally's graph. In whose graph do you
see an immaculate home? Not mine! Where on that graph
would I put an immaculate home? I'm not at the baseline
long enough to dust. An immaculate home is definitely in the
Everything category. To make sure everyone knows that *I*
know my house isn't immaculate and it's OK with me, I have
a beautifully framed art piece in my kitchen that says, "Dull
women have immaculate homes." No one has ever accused me
of being dull.

I do have a pretty home. I love beauty and order, and I
believe that he or she who dies with the most antique furniture
wins. I don't care if it has dust on it. I want it because its
beauty inspires me. It is a rush when I find it, when it arrives
at my house, and when I get up every morning and marvel at
its luscious curves and carvings.

Look at the two graphs again. In whose graph do you see
gourmet meals? Not mine! At my house a tuna fish salad
sandwich with lettuce is a four-course meal (1. bread; 2. tuna;
3. lettuce; 4. bread—see? four courses). All is having dinner

together as a family. The meal itself might give Martha Stewart a rash, but we'll suffer through it as a team.

## The Garden of Eden It's Not

Another woman told me that she cleared up a big source of frustration by applying the All versus Everything test. She said she loved having a garden but could not find the time to keep it up and the weeds gave her more stress than the flowers gave her pleasure. In addition, the pressure to keep up with the Joneses (who had a gorgeous garden) kept her awake at night. She said, "One day I declared, 'Having my own garden is Everything. Enjoying the neighbors' garden is having it All.'" Now she lets them plant and weed to their hearts' content while she relaxes and enjoys the fruits of their labor.

Dr. Joyce Brothers, in her book *The Successful Woman*, talked about her version of All versus Everything. Like many women, she lamented that her husband would not push a vacuum cleaner if the floor were knee-deep in dust. She said essentially that she had filed her husband's vacuuming under Everything. Getting her husband to sweep would cause a lot of disconnection. All, she concluded, was being together and staying connected. "It is far more important to me that we spend what time we have together happily, not bickering over trivia like dusting and bed making. For they truly are trivia when compared with the rest that life has to offer. If you weigh dust kittens under the bed against laughter, and dirty dishes in the sink against good sex, laughter and sex, in my book, win out every time."

I am not, of course, suggesting that men shouldn't vacuum. I am implying that each of us has to decide what is really important, to pick our battles based on getting what we really want, and to make sure the battles are worth fighting.

## The Cream of the Crop

I often ask my audience members to make a chart of their All versus Everything list. Here are some of my favorites:

| **"Everything" would be:** | **I'd have it "All" if I had:** |
| --- | --- |
| A place for everything and everything in its place | Closets with doors that close |
| A tall, dark, handsome man to love me | A loyal dog that loves me and doesn't talk back |
| Having everyone understand my moods and situations | A true best friend to share things with |
| A perfectly scrubbed house | Traffic patterns |
| The Instant Baby-sitter—just add water when you need one | Fun taking my toddler to the older kid's events |

Deb Kromer of Castalia, Ohio, said it best: "Having Everything would be watching the reflection of a full moon shimmer in the waters of the French Riviera off a seventy-foot yacht. Having it All is watching the fireflies at dusk while Daddy helps five-year-old Shelby pitch her new pup tent in our backyard."

Beautiful. Deb does have it All.

## The Ever-Changing List

When you make yourself a list of the All versus Everything items in your life, remember that the list is not static. Just because something appears on the Everything list now doesn't mean it can't someday show up on the All list.

For example, I got married in the seventies, in our "earthy" period, when I would not have considered owning anything as decadent as a diamond. We bought $50 silver rings engraved with the markings of a sixteenth-century chalice (we're talking really earthy here). Well, I'm not in my earthy period any more. I'd say I'm very comfortable in my decadently materialistic phase, and I would love to have a beautiful diamond ring the size of a hubcap with matching necklace, earrings, and bracelet. One of my friends suggested I get a diamond for my fifteenth wedding anniversary. I thought, well, the first anniversary is the paper anniversary, and the ninth is lace. I told her I'd love to get a diamond. Let's see, it looks like the fifteenth is the orthodontic anniversary, so all three kids will be getting braces. Guess it'll have to wait. It won't wait forever. Someday I'll dazzle and blind passersby with my jewelry. But first my kids will dazzle the world with their smile. And that is All.

## THE NEW SOLUTION:
## HAVING IT ALL

*When we can't keep up, we have a choice. We can:*

| DISCONNECT | CONNECT |
|---|---|
| **Strive for Everything**<br>I've just got to lose twenty pounds before the class reunion or I'm not going. | **Strive for it All**<br>I'm going to lose ten pounds and buy a suit that hides the other ten. I want to have fun with my old classmates. |
| **Feel stressed**<br>I need to get a second job so we can take the kids on a big vacation. | **Feel satisfied**<br>The kids are only three and five. We can have more fun every evening if I'm home instead of working. |

| Be persnickety | Be playful |
|---|---|
| These toys all over the place are driving me crazy. I am ready to throw them in the trash. | "I am going to count to 25 and whoever has the most toys put away gets to pick out the book we'll read before naptime." |

## MICROACTIONS

1. Draw your ideal life-balance graph and compare it to reality.
2. Make a list of the All versus Everything items in your life.
3. Do the items on your All list help connect you to yourself or someone important in your life?
4. Talk to your family about their ideas on the subject.
5. Ask yourself, "What kind of life makes me glad to get up in the morning and glad to go to bed at night?" What do you need to make it happen?
6. How could you get something that is on the Everything list onto the All list?
7. How is your All versus Everything list different from your partner's list?

## IN REAL LIFE

Dear Mary,

I took your course "Achieving Harmony: Balancing Your Personal and Professional Life."

For me, All is having things organized so I am able to find what I need. Everything is having EVERYTHING organized in PERFECT ORDER.

Last summer vacation, I organized my classroom for

seven of the eight weeks and ended up not having much of a summer break. After about a month of teaching, I felt disorganized again! I learned the hard way I could spend FOREVER organizing and still not be totally organized. Now I strive for All, not Everything.

Thank you for teaching me about life balance and connections.

Mahalo,

Theresa Lynn Johnson

Kailua, Oahu

# CHAPTER 13

# Don't Do Something; Just Sit There

*Whatever success I have had may perhaps be
attributable to three things. One is silence;
the second is more silence; while the third
is still more silence.*

—*Ivar Kreuger*

Fast is the name of the game. Many corporations list
"speed" as part of their mission statement. The business world
believes Will Rogers's adage, "Even if you are on the right
track, if you just stand there you are going to get run over."
And they are right. In business if you snooze you lose. It is
pointless to tell people to slow down. They have a dozen valid
reasons why they can't.

I actually like going fast. I was born eight weeks premature.
My mother said I was in a hurry to get here and I have been
in a hurry ever since.

On the other hand, cemeteries and hospitals are full of people who got there in a hurry, way ahead of the much slower
crowd. So are those our two choices? Lose out to our faster

competition or have a heart attack staying on top? I believe we can go fast if we take the time to . . . pause.

## The Pause That Refreshes

I hired a wonderful speaking coach, Lou Heckler, to improve my platform skills. He gave me professional tips that helped immensely. One piece of advice I had a hard time accepting, however, was his suggestion that I slow down, especially in the critical stories. I didn't want to slow down. I really liked going at a fast clip. I could give the audience more information, and I feared I would lose them if I took too much time lingering over a point or two. Lou kept insisting the audience wouldn't mind if I took extra time to "plant the seeds really deep." I was skeptical.

A few months later, I spoke to an audience of two thousand people. Before going onstage, in my imagination I sat my coach on my shoulder and said, "So, Lou, my man, what do I need to know today?" He said, "Just have fun."

And we did. I was relaxed and confident and the most amazing thing happened. I . . . paused.

I actually stood on stage and said nothing. In between stories, in the middle of stories, in the middle of sentences. Silence. I just let the story sink in. The audience loved it. I loved it. The longer I waited the more we laughed and the more fun we had.

I wrote to my coach. "There is one drawback to this pause technique. You can't cram in nearly as much material when you are pausing, laughing and having a good time. I guess I'll just have to learn to live with it."

Reading my own words, I understood that the principle applies to life in general. When we *pause*—in speeches or in life—we can't cram in nearly as much "material," but we laugh and have so much fun, we don't even notice what we are "missing." If only we would take an occasional respite. Ironically, I was just as successful, just as productive, when I stopped to take a breath as when I spoke at the speed of light.

Keep in mind that I didn't have to slow down—I just took a little break. And I didn't have to wait until I got to a good stopping point. In fact, pausing in the middle of the story, often when the audience least expected it, had the most impact.

I try to pause more. Sometimes I am still a miserable failure at it. One December I had the honor of hosting three of my new friends from England. I was busy racing around, getting everything just so. They had been such delightful hosts when I visited their home that I was knocking myself out to return the favor.

Now, what are the English going to want in the afternoon? Tea, of course. I purchased special English tea and brought out my best china. With great pride I served them the finest tea party I could muster.

They seemed less than delighted. I reasoned, "It's probably just because English people are a little reserved, or maybe they're jet-lagged from the long trip over." The next day I served them tea again, and although they were polite, they seemed to be sharing sideways glances.

I know you will be as surprised to learn this as I was: The English do not like their tea . . . microwaved! They don't even use tea bags. Apparently, it's considered very bad manners to have that little tag hanging over the side of your cup. They had no idea what to do with it. I blew their minds.

Being the hostess with the mostest, I kept offering to warm it back up. "Can I pop it back in the microwave for you?"

Suddenly I realized, "They think I'm from Mars or at the very least an international diplomat's nightmare." I had no idea how talented I am: I can insult an entire country in just a party or two.

Actually, I am just American. I get rewarded for accomplishing jobs *fast*. Just nuke the water, stir the bag around five times, and slug down the tea standing at the counter. There. You wanted tea? I can give you an entire tea party in eighty-five seconds. I apologized, and they laughed. (I think they were laughing.) They explained that tea takes time to brew, that you have to *sit down*. Having a proper cup of tea is a process. In fact, that is the whole point of the afternoon tea ritual. Their culture has a built-in pause mechanism.

## A New Year's Resolution

Did you make your New Year's resolutions with the hope that *this* year you'll keep your life in balance? I always make a list of lofty goals, things I want to achieve, possess, and experience. In 1997 I added a different activity to help me connect. My friend, Dr. Bill Garrett, inspired me to take a new approach.

Bill is an astute observer and listener. I am amazed at how he will sit patiently and listen to a group discuss a topic and then (what seems like) out of the blue, he will make the most profound statement that clarifies the issue succinctly and brilliantly. I asked him how he learned to do this.

Bill told me, "The first day of my internship the chief resident warned our anxious group of medical interns that we would be the first ones called at night to resuscitate a patient whose heart had stopped. The chief resident advised us, 'You will all live in fear of that dreaded call. And when it comes in the middle of the night, after you have rushed to the patient's bedside and observed everyone crashing in with carts and EKG machines and resuscitation equipment the very *first thing* you should do is . . .' "

take your own pulse.

I really like that strategy. We often think we must make an immediate decision, get into action—*do* something. In times of crisis, big or small, imagine how much better things might turn out if we just stopped, looked around for a moment, and then took our own pulse. Sure, there are times when we have to act in a split second. But even in life-and-death circumstances, sometimes the prudent thing to *do* is

Wait . . .
Think . . .
Count.

And let's be honest. Real "life and death" decisions are rare—even in most medical professions. Many of our "crises" are self-made, transitory, and trivial. Before we nag our spouse, criticize our kids, tailgate that jerk on the highway; before we get snippy with the rude clerk, fume at the slow line, or get impatient with our aging parent . . . maybe we could mentally, if not literally, take our own pulse.

It's a New Year's resolution worth keeping.

## SHHHHHHHH! I Can't Hear You

As much as many of us hate to slow down, we struggle even more with silence.

The TV serves as background noise, the radio blares in the car, and we jog with headphones. Our fax machines, cellular phones, and pagers tap and ring and beep. The alarm clock wakes us up with a prison-raid siren, and late-night TV puts us to sleep. We live in a very noisy world. Anne Morrow Lindbergh, author of *Gift from the Sea*, wrote, "We seem so frightened of being alone that we never let it happen. . . . Instead of planting our solitude with our dream blossoms, we choke the space with continuous music, chatter and companionship to which we do not even listen. It is simply there to fill the vacuum. When the noise stops there is no inner music to take its place. We must relearn to be alone."

> "Dear God, Please shout your answers. You know
> how stubborn you made me!" (Valerie Eichenberg)

Since pausing and experiencing silence don't come naturally to most of us, we need a technique to draw them into our life. I was wrestling with a long-standing problem and expressed my frustration to my dear friend, Brenda Abdilla.

She asked, "Have you spent any time really thinking about this problem?"

"Thinking about it! Are you kidding? That's all I've thought of for months!"

She smiled. "No, I'm not talking about obsessing and worrying. I mean *quiet contemplation.*" She recommended I try the following reflection that she read about in *God in All Things* by Anthony de Mello. This is my adaptation of the meditation:

> Find a quiet spot.
> Take a few deep breaths.
> Relax your muscles.
> Close your eyes.
> Breathe deeply.

Now picture going up an escalator. At the top, doors open and you step into a beautiful lush green field. See yourself sitting on the grass. Feel the warm sunshine on your face. Notice the gentle breeze. Feel the peace around you. You are relaxed and happy.

A beautiful stream runs in front of you. Across the stream, sitting on the grass, you notice _____. (Here you insert the person or force you want to talk to. Depending on your beliefs, you might select: Jesus, Buddha, Mother Earth, Socrates, a deceased relative, Mohammed, Abraham Lincoln, Martin Luther King, the Virgin Mary, the universe, etc.)

You see the Teacher beckoning to you to cross the stream. You step into the water. It is deep and that person or force reaches out to help you across. When you reach the other side, you sit on the grass together. He or she takes your hand and says, "Never be afraid to reach out to me." You look directly into the face of your teacher, and you explain your concerns, pouring out all that is bothering you.

Then you ask for guidance, and . . . listen.

I cannot begin to tell you the wisdom and insight I have gained with this meditation. I received answers that solved my problems in ways I had never before considered. Shortly after I began my company, Life Balance, Inc., I began having doubts about my ability to succeed in this brand new and intensely competitive endeavor. Thinking, What have I got to lose? I tried Brenda's meditation.

I found the meadow, saw my Teacher, crossed the stream, and sat down with Him. I explained my fears and insecurities. Finishing, I asked, "I'm trying to create a new business based on helping people find harmony through connection. I am putting tons of energy (and money) into it. So let's start at the beginning. Am I even supposed to be doing this?"

I waited and . . . listened.

I heard the answer quite clearly. I do not believe my subconscious would have come up with this response on its own.

He replied, "Mary, it is why I sent you."

I started to cry because I knew His words were true. Whenever I have renewed doubts and fears about my mission, I remind myself, "It is why I am here."

I taught my children this problem-solving method. They seemed to like it but did not say much. One day my teenage daughter stormed in crying, and ran to her room.

Concerned, I knocked on her door. "Sarah, what's wrong?"

"Nothing!" she sobbed.

I tapped again. "I'm here if you need to talk."

She opened the door a crack and said, "It's OK, Mom. I'll just go across the stream."

Real balance originates in connection. Connecting with ourselves through prayer, meditation, or simply allowing ourselves to let the chatter quiet down is a path we must not underestimate.

## Feel Good Files

Another activity you might enjoy while you are "just sitting there and doing nothing" is to dip into your Feel Good File. A Feel Good File is just what it sounds like—a place to keep all those cards, letters, pictures, performance ratings, cartoons, and other mementos that warm your heart. You might include a dried flower from a wedding, a picture of your motorcycle, or the Rod Stewart concert ticket stubs.

A Feel Good File reminds you about your joys, your loves, your adventures—your connections in this world. It is an ancient concept found in many cultures. The Native Americans carried around objects in a deerskin medicine bag, believing that remembering was good medicine for the soul.

## Ward Off Evil Spirits

Keep one at work. We all have days when we feel frustrated and rejected, when someone stomps into our office, kicks us in the teeth, and stomps out. Just open up your folder and remind yourself of your past successes. Keep one at home, too. When you are in the mood for some stillness, let your cache fill your soul.

## It Can Save Your Dog's Life

Feel Good Files make ideal gifts. Your family and friends will thank you over and over. I sent one as a gift to a meeting planner, Cathy Carballada, of Cleveland, Ohio. A few days later I received this reply:

> Dear Mary,
> Thank you so much for the feel good file. I received it today. I have to tell you, it saved my dog's life. As I opened my mail this evening I found your letter in the file. I felt really great about it. I looked up. In our hallway, I see shreds of paper. On closer examination, I found that they are pieces of my bathroom wallpaper! Apparently my puppy, CJ, is in her second chewing stage. I thought about killing her but I knew that would really throw my life off balance. My husband and I had a great laugh and I wanted you to know that I am putting a piece of wallpaper into my file because it will make me laugh on sight.

Now here's a woman who truly understands the spirit of the Feel Good File.

## Thirty-Two Cents Can Make You Feel Like a Million

My husband, Joe, who is a high school counselor, came home physically and emotionally exhausted from working all day with stepparents and their kids. He blurted out in frustration, "I've never seen it work. I've never seen a stepparent function as a real parent. The dynamics are mind-boggling!"

When we get overwhelmed and exhausted we often say things we do not mean. In the middle of this ridiculous statement he said, "Except, of course, for our good friend Matt. He is a gentle and loving stepfather. He treats his daughters with respect like any good father would—step or otherwise."

The next day I wrote Matt Warren a little note, relaying the compliment he had received from my husband. A few weeks later Matt's wife, Jackie, phoned me, "I had to call and tell you. Your letter just made Matt's day. And most importantly, he brought the letter home to me. When I read it I started to cry. The letter reminded me that this man had come into my life and not only did he love me, but he loved my children as well, embracing them as his own. I realized that I hadn't said 'thank you' in a very long time. We sat down and talked about the fact that we had created the family that both of us had always wanted."

I shared her remarks with Joe and we both felt like we'd been given a million bucks. About a year later, Matt and Jackie attended my seminar. Matt bought each family member a Feel Good File. He showed them to me and smiled, "I want you to know the first thing I am going to put in is your note."

He had saved that card for a year! It made him feel good when he first opened it and it continues to remind him that he is indeed a fabulous father.

Thirty-two cents and five minutes of my time gave the four of us joy. Do you understand the power that we have to make each other feel good? Do you understand that it is that exact same power you can use to make yourself feel good any time you want to by focusing on the things in your Feel Good File? Imagine, all that just by sitting and doing nothing.

## Who Says It Won't Work in Business?

I read an article by Tom Peters, the management guru, on sending business thank-you notes. He commented on a hand-written note he had received from a fellow who had attended one of his programs. The gentleman wrote, "Nice job! Thought you might enjoy the attached." The "attached" was an article out of a local newspaper on a subject that Tom had gotten worked up about during his speech.

Tom wrote, "You know what, I've reread his scribble a couple of times, and I'll probably put it in my save box. 'Nice job!' No big deal? Well, it is to me."

I read the article twice to make sure I had it right. His "save box"? He would keep the tiny note?

Tom Peters has a Feel Good File! Yes!


## No Longer Surprised

One day my family was playing one of those question games and my father was asked, "If your house was on fire and you could save only one material possession, what would it be?"

I was sure I knew his answer. Probably his golf clubs. Maybe his father's pocket watch.

He quickly answered. "My drawer."

"What drawer?"

"In the bureau in the upstairs bedroom where I save all the letters and cards you kids send me."

My father's most prized possession is a feel good drawer! You could have knocked me over with a feather.


## Why Do They Work?

The scientist in me always wants to know why the strategies work. When I received Lainie Teshima's letter I understood. She wrote,

Oh! That Feel Good File is just GREAT! I compiled all the positive letters I kept tucked away and put them in a special file. I have a collection of letters from my students and parents. Whenever I start to feel like I am not doing that good of a job teaching, I open up my file and read some of those letters. It's a great picker-upper. The letters are so touching because they bring back memories of the year and bring tears to my eyes. Boy, just reading those letters makes me feel worthy again.

We all want to belong and know what we do makes a difference. Let your Feel Good File lift you up. Try taking a magical, renewing pause. Or simply listen to the silence. Tap into the power of connection—with yourself.

## THE NEW SOLUTION: CONNECTING TO THE BIG PICTURE

*When we can't keep up, we have a choice. We can:*

| DISCONNECT | CONNECT |
| --- | --- |
| **Experience clamor** I'm so far behind. I've got to work faster. | **Embrace silence** I think I'll take a pause and reenergize. |
| **Obsess about our problems** I don't know what to do! I tried everything. | **Listen for answers to our problems** I'll try quiet contemplation and listen. |
| **Respond to chaos** Why is everyone hollering at me? I can't stand this place anymore! | **Reclaim solitude** I think I'll close the door and dip into my Feel Good File. |

The most enlightened people of all time meditated, prayed, and used silence regularly to make their great contributions to humanity. It is especially important in today's noisy, high-tech world to find quiet places and quiet times where we can let our minds run freely. "It is during such times," wrote Samuel Cypert, "that our best ideas come. If Archimedes had been watching *Wheel of Fortune* on his portable TV while he was in the bath, our math skills might still be in the dark ages."

We are no different. Make a commitment today to give yourself permission to pause and practice daily silence. Connect with the big picture.

## MICROACTIONS

1. Don't answer the phone for an hour a day. Try it for one hour per day for one week. What happened during that hour?
2. Start a Feel Good File today.
3. Write in a journal. If you are new at this, just write on the first day of the month or one day a week and see what comes out.
4. Sit alone in the backyard. Listen. What do you hear? See? Feel? Sense?
5. Sit still for ten minutes. No people, no activity, no extraneous noise. Just listen.
6. Schedule a three-minute meditation/prayer time for yourself once a week. Write down what you thought about.
7. Try going across the stream.

## IN REAL LIFE

Dear Mary,

I felt "ready" to write to you because I've tried microactions and do you know what? They actually work! I have two sons, Tyler, who is six going on twelve, and Tanner, eight months. Well, I don't have to tell you how "challenging" it is to keep everything together. After class, I thought, "Do I want everything, or do I want it all?"

I always felt compelled to keep everything going and in the process didn't realize how I wasn't appreciating my two sons. Being totally exhausted, mentally, physically, and emotionally at the end of the day, what do I have left for my family or more importantly, for myself?

I took it one microaction at a time. I decided, instead of coming home and running to the kitchen to start dinner or to the laundry room to start the laundry, I would just sit still! WOW! It was strange. I just sat on the sofa, Tyler in a daze staring at me wondering if I was OK. I just sat and calmly watched with enjoyment as Tanner gleefully crawled on the floor with wonder and curiosity, looking for something to invade or destroy or investigate. Unfortunately it was the vertical blinds. In any other situation, I would have come running into the living room yelling, "No! No!" But for some reason I just watched him viciously yank and pull at the blinds. His expression was priceless. He was very pleased and satisfied with what he had discovered, the noise it makes, the way it feels. It was awesome! (I was also very pleased with what I had discovered: Enjoy the little things and the little people in your life because they don't stay little forever.) The clattering lasted for about three minutes. Then it stopped. Tanner was satisfied. He moved on to his next victim, the television remote control.

As my attention turned to Tyler, who at this point had lost interest in watching me just sit on the sofa, I wondered what was going through his head as he meticulously chose his super action figures. When his collection was complete, he began thrashing the figures, complete with terrific surround-sound Dolby stereo effects. He quickly glanced my way and curiously asked if I wanted to play. We played for about five minutes until our battle of good versus evil was abruptly interrupted by you guessed it—Tanner!!!

The dinner had to be made, the clothes had to be washed, but they waited. They waited twenty minutes until Tyler was ready, until Tanner was ready, until I was ready. The daily chores could wait but my two boys couldn't. Why should they have to?

Thanks for a great class.

Todi Otsuka

Mililani, Hawaii

# CHAPTER 14

# The Power of Connecting

*Never lose sight of the fact that the most important yardstick of your success will be how you treat other people—your family, friends, and coworkers and even strangers you meet along the way.*

—*Barbara Bush*

My mother was only nine years old when she lost her mother to cancer. My grandfather turned to alcohol in his grief and was unable to care for his four daughters. The state put my mother and her sisters in foster care. In those days "the system" was not very careful about screening foster parents. The first home was quite abusive and the two older sisters ran away. My aunt Gladys, only four years old, and my mother lived apart in separate homes.

My mother rarely talked about her childhood. It almost seemed like her life story began when she married my dad.

In 1995 I interviewed my seventy-year-old mother, Lou, in a review of her life and videotaped the conversation. (See Chapter 7.) I asked her, "What is the hardest thing you ever faced?"

I wondered what the answer would be. My mother had

many challenges in her lifetime: growing up without a mother; suffering several miscarriages and losing a child at birth; raising six children, one with a serious mental handicap; and temporarily losing her hearing because of a side effect of medication. Unfortunately, she had a long list from which to choose.

She paused and with tears in her eyes she whispered, "Not growing up with my sisters."

It was the first time I ever realized how painful that must have been. With five brothers of my own, I took for granted the sense of connection I felt with all of them. I did not understand how lucky I was to really know them. I also fully realized for the first time that my mother did not have this sense of belonging in her childhood. I felt helpless to change her situation and wondered about all the other foster children just like her.

## But What Could I do?

Then I received the following letter from Lynn Price, detailing her feelings about growing up as a foster child:

> Dear Mary,
>
> I have a confession to make. When I attended one of your sessions and was introduced to you, I was very apprehensive. After all, I heard that you talked about June Cleaver, balance, connection, and creating family memories. I was very nervous because I certainly did not grow up in the Cleaver family!
>
> I was placed in foster care as an infant when my mother was institutionalized with mental illness and my father abandoned me. I did not know that I was a foster child nor that I had a biological sister until age eight, when my parents sat me down and said, "We're not your real

parents." You see, my birth mother had made a miraculous "recovery" and insisted on visitation. Switching worlds between my foster family and my biological mother was a terrible strain. When it came to my mother, I only thought of all the years she wasn't there and how bitter she was about the past, filling me with guilt. As for my natural father, I learned only last year that he was not my father and that I was actually born through artificial insemination.

So you can imagine, as I waited for your talk, I thought I was setting myself up for depression, self-inflicted pressure to make something positive of my past and make up for my childhood by giving more to my children.

Well, I was pleasantly surprised as I learned I could apply June Cleaver, life balance, connection, and memories as it pertains to my own definition of family. Your memory video became a bonding experience as I chose to create the heirloom with my in-laws, which flattered them and touched my husband. Your Memory Jar became a treasure to me when my friends who are like family to me gathered on my fortieth birthday and highlighted so many of the wonderful times we shared. Your ideas for connecting with my children, even in the midst of chaos, have proven invaluable.

Your strategies have helped me look at family in a whole new fulfilling way. And, in the process, I've learned to focus differently on family as it pertains to the past, and I've tried not to be so perfect as it relates to memories. I learned that when giving treasures of life balance, it feels just as wonderful for the giver as it does for the recipient.

I want you to know that your talk on connection and

belonging inspired me to name the camp I have founded. Camp To Belong is a nonprofit, all-volunteer organization that holds events so foster children can be reunited with siblings who have been placed, as my sister Andi and I were, in different homes. The first camp was held in Las Vegas, and believe me, seeing those children cling to their natural brothers and sisters, I understood what you meant when you said, "Real balance originates in connection."

Thanks again for showing me a wonderful way to reflect on the family I have made for myself.

Best regards,

Lynn Price

Las Vegas, Nevada

---

I was moved by her sincere wish to make Camp To Belong a reality. I called her, and she told me about the plight of the 500,000 American children in foster care. She told me almost 85 percent of them have at least one sibling and 75 percent of them are separated when placed in homes. She explained her plans to build a national nonprofit organization dedicated to reuniting the siblings at events including a one-week overnight camp. She also wanted to establish a communication system so the kids could stay in touch.

I quickly remembered my mom and then imagined my own three children orphaned and separated.

I knew my answer had come. When Lynn held the first camp in 1995 my mother and I sponsored two sisters. What an emotional experience for us! I told my mother that I felt like we were sending nine-year-old Lou and little Gladys to camp together. She smiled.

I had the honor of attending the camp this year. Held in the beautiful Rocky Mountains, seventy-seven lucky kids spent a week of fun, adventure, and camaraderie with their biological siblings. For some, this was the only time of the year they see their brother or sister.

On the last night of camp, the kids performed a talent show. Midway through the program, a thirteen-year-old boy took the stage, asked his nine-year-old sister to join him, and with his arm snugly around her shoulder he sang, "Stand by Me." They shared a magical night, knowing they belonged to each other.

I looked over at my daughter Emily and tears were streaming down her face. I realized then what enormous power we have to make a difference in our own lives, as well as others, through connection.

I thought I was powerless to help my mother. Lynn Price and the kids of Camp To Belong taught me I *do* have the power. I am now their national spokesperson. (For information on the camp, see page 235.) My involvement brings me such joy. No matter how busy I am, I discover I am never too swamped to reach out and let the kids make me feel good.

## You Have the Power, Too!

Thank you for taking this journey with me. I hope you, too, believe that connection creates balance and that you have found many usable ideas to make this principle work for you in real life. From now on, when you get out of kilter, instead of saying, "What do I need to do?" I hope you will ask instead, "With whom should I connect?" More important, I want you to say to yourself, "You know, I am not really so out of balance. I already do many of these strategies in one form or another. I am actually quite connected. I relate, bond, and get turned on. I am committed to focusing even more on connection. Maybe it is time to give myself some credit for all the good I do."

It most certainly *is* time. Our situations are imperfect. We probably won't live the Cleaver life. We can't get it all done. But, we do have the power to keep our lives in balance.

All we have to do is . . .

Connect!

# I Would Love to Hear from You!

I would be delighted to know what connection strategies work for you. Please send me your ideas, stories, insights, and feedback. Reach me at:

Mary LoVerde MS ANP
Life Balance, Inc.
25066 E. Plymouth Circle
Aurora, CO 80016
303-766-9547
Connect597@aol.com
www.maryloverde.com

## Information on Camp To Belong

Camp To Belong is a nonprofit, all-volunteer organization dedicated to reuniting siblings placed in separate foster homes for times of fun, feeling, and emotional empowerment. The main events include a one-week summer overnight camp and quarterly reunions. Camp To Belong also strives to educate the nation about the plight of foster siblings and the need to keep them together in foster care (or adoption) whenever possible.

Founded by Lynn Price in March 1995 in Las Vegas, Nevada, Camp To Belong has expanded to Colorado and Illinois. Her vision is to establish regional camps and reunions across the country, encourage use of the toll-free support line and Website, and develop written and video materials to tell the story of foster siblings.

Ms. Price, executive director, and her sister Andi Andree, director, from Sycamore, Illinois, spent a majority of their childhood in foster care in separate homes. They did not meet until Lynn was eight and Andi was nine, and it took them many years to develop a relationship as sisters. Today, as moms, wives, and professional women, they are best friends and do not want other foster siblings to miss the opportunity to share their young years and build a successful adult life.

For more information or to make a donation:

Camp To Belong
9445 South Sand Hill Place
Highlands Ranch, CO 80126
303-791-0915
Fax: 303-791-0916;
Website: www.camptobelong.org

## Product Ordering Information

All the ideas in this book are possible without buying anything. Thousands of people have created their own Memory Jars and family videos. Still, many people have urged me to have some ready-made products to make the projects easier. If you would like information on how to purchase these products please write, e-mail or fax me at the address on page 235.

## The Memory Jar Kit (Chapter 7)

When you want to give the perfect gift for Mother's Day, Father's Day, Christmas, Hanukkah, anniversaries, birthdays, retirements, weddings, and reunions . . . create a Memory Jar! The Memory Jar kit includes a beautiful custom-designed frosted etched glass jar with a package of decorative cards that say *"I remember . . ."* on the front and are blank inside for you to write your thoughts. The recipient will feel loved and appreciated as they read and reread the warm, funny, and touching memories written on each *"I remember"* Memory Jar card. You may also order the jar or cards separately.

## Touching Tomorrow (Chapter 7)

What does your mother remember about her first kiss? What's the first thing your father tells himself every morning? By the time we are adults, it is all too easy to look at our parents and grandparents as though their causing a communication and generation gap seemingly impossible to bridge. But the older we get, the more we understand the importance of connecting with our elders before they're gone. There is no better way to do this than to talk to them like you never have before and create a record of their lives to share with the next generation.

Touching Tomorrow contains everything you need to record your family's most valuable asset: their wisdom, humor, and love. It features more than two hundred questions that are sure to help you know your loved ones better than you ever dreamed, tips on preparing both yourself and your elders for the technical and emotional process, helpful hints on coaxing shy or reluctant family members to participate, and heartwarming real-life stories from people who have already preserved their elders' memories on tape. This is an invaluable guide to creating a precious family heirloom—one that will truly touch tomorrow.

## Your Family's Greatest Gift (Chapter 7)

The greatest gift a family can give itself is a sense of belonging. Feel the joy of belonging to your special family by capturing your elders' wisdom and stories on videotape. This booklet includes everything you need to make family memories last forever. It includes the questions to ask, interviewing and videotaping tips, heartwarming editing suggestions, how to overcome the interviewee's shyness and resistance, and the cost of the project.